I0124774

EU Cohesion
Policy in Practice

ROWMAN & LITTLEFIELD
INTERNATIONAL—POLICY IMPACTS

The Rowman & Littlefield International—Policy Impacts series aims to bridge the gap between the academic community and policymakers: providing academics with a format and channel for policy-relevant research and ensuring that policymakers are informed about the best research available to them. Rowman & Littlefield International—Policy Impacts provides a forum for knowledge exchange, a bank of information and a toolkit for implementation.

Titles in the Series:

EU Cohesion Policy in Practice

What Does it Achieve?

John Bachtler, Iain Begg,
David Charles and Laura Polverari

ROWMAN & LITTLEFIELD
INTERNATIONAL
London • New York

Published by Rowman & Littlefield International, Ltd.
Unit A, Whitacre Mews, 26-34 Stannary Street, London SE11 4AB
www.rowmaninternational.com

Rowman & Littlefield International, Ltd. is an affiliate of
Rowman & Littlefield
4501 Forbes Boulevard, Suite 200, Lanham, Maryland 20706, USA
With additional offices in Boulder, New York, Toronto (Canada), and Plymouth (UK)
www.rowman.com

Copyright © 2016 John Bachtler, Iain Begg, David Charles and Laura Polverari

All rights reserved. No part of this book may be reproduced in any form or by
any electronic or mechanical means, including information storage and retrieval
systems, without written permission from the publisher, except by a reviewer who
may quote passages in a review.

British Library Cataloguing in Publication Data
A catalogue record for this book is available from the British Library

ISBN: HB 978-1-78348-721-9
        PB 978-1-78348-722-6

Library of Congress Cataloging-in-Publication Data

Names: Bachtler, John, author.
Title: EU cohesion policy in practice : what does it achieve? / John
    Bachtler, Iain Begg, David Charles and Laura Polverari.
Other titles: European Union cohesion policy in practice
Description: London ; New York : Rowman & Littlefield International, 2016. |
    Series: Policy impacts | Includes bibliographical references and index.
Identifiers: LCCN 2016010393 (print) | LCCN 2016022806 (ebook) | ISBN
    9781783487219 (cloth : alk. paper) | ISBN 9781783487226 (pbk. : alk.
    paper) | ISBN 9781783487233 (Electronic)
Subjects: LCSH: Structural adjustment (Economic policy)—European Union
    countries. | Regional planning—European Union countries. | European Union
    countries—Economic integration. | European Union countries—Regional
    disparities.
Classification: LCC HC240 .B243 2016 (print) | LCC HC240 (ebook) | DDC
    338.94—dc23
LC record available at https://lccn.loc.gov/2016010393

∞™ The paper used in this publication meets the minimum requirements of
American National Standard for Information Sciences—Permanence of Paper
for Printed Library Materials, ANSI/NISO Z39.48-1992.

Printed in the United States of America

Contents

List of Tables, Figures and Boxes

TABLES

FIGURES

BOX

Preface

Over past two decades there have been extensive efforts to assess the achievements, effectiveness and impact of the European Union's Cohesion policy. These have varied with regard to the scope of the research, the empirical questions formulated and the methodological approaches adopted. Consequently, there is little consensus among researchers on these questions, and the results vary depending on the methodology used, the time period considered or the unit of analysis. Further, due to the changing policy focus over time and to the different foci of the studies undertaken, the outcomes of research and evaluation cannot be easily aggregated to obtain a cumulative vision of the policy's achievements.

This study takes a fresh look at the achievements of Cohesion policy, adopting a distinctive methodological approach. It uses theory-based evaluation to assess the relevance, effectiveness and utility of European Regional Development Fund (ERDF) programmes implemented in fifteen case-study regions across the EU15 over the period from 1989 to 2012, covering almost five complete programme periods.

Any longitudinal analysis of Cohesion policy faces formidable difficulties given that even expenditure data become increasingly sparse as one goes back into early programme periods, and the specification and recording of physical outcomes are incomplete and often unreliable. It is also challenging to reconstruct the logic of programmes, especially as the stated objectives and priorities frequently differ from the implicit purpose of programmes as revealed through the allocation of resources to projects. However, by taking a long-term perspective, it becomes possible to see the evolution of regional development strategies—their conceptual basis, rationale, strategic objectives, priorities and implementation arrangements—and to understand effects that transcend specific programme periods, or that may not show up in regional indicators such as GDP growth or unemployment.

This study originated in a project commissioned by the Evaluation Unit of the Directorate-General for Regional and Urban Policy in the European Commission, undertaken jointly by the European Policies Research Centre (EPRC, University of Strathclyde, Glasgow) and the London School of Economics (LSE). It was conducted by the authors of this volume together with research colleagues at EPRC and LSE, supplemented by research associates who undertook fieldwork research and analysis for specific regions.

We are grateful to Professor Riccardo Crescenzi, Dr. Ugo Fratesi and Dr. Vassilis Monastiriotis of LSE for their research contribution to the study, including the analysis of needs in chapter 4 and table 4.2 (Vassilis Monastiriotis) and the quantitative analysis of needs in chapter 7 and figures 7.1–7.3 (Ugo Fratesi). We also acknowledge with appreciation the contributions of the regional research teams including Cosmin Bolea, Cristina Calvo-Porral, Pascal Chazaud, Victoria Chorafa, Niall Crosbie, Heikki Eskelinen, Professor Andrés Faíña, José Fernández-Serrano, Jim Fitzpatrick, Estelle Floirac, Matti Fritsch, Markus Gruber, Professor Marina Gruševaja, Professor Gerhard Heimpold, Timo Hirvonen, Stephan Kupsa, Dimitris Lianos, Jesús López-Rodríguez, Georges Mercier, Rona Michie, Dr. Simona Milio, Paulino Montes-Solla, Delphine Paumelle, Simon Pohn-Weidinger, Isidoro Romero, Professor Regina Salvador, Pasi Saukkonen, Dr. Oliver Schwab, Dr. Kristin Schwarze, Brendan Shiels, Ricardo Simões, Laura Tagle and Laura Todaro.

More broadly we would like to thank all those who participated in the research: interviewees, survey respondents, participants in the regional workshops, external experts and other stakeholders who contributed to the research in various ways.

Last but not least, we are grateful to Veronica Gaffey (former head of the DG Regio Evaluation Unit) and her colleagues, José Luis Calvo de Celis and Kai Stryczynski, for the funding of the study and for the stimulating intellectual and methodological debates that accompanied the research process. The opinions expressed and any errors remain, of course, our own.

John Bachtler, Iain Begg, David Charles, Laura Polverari
December 2015

Chapter One

Introduction

Understanding the Effectiveness of EU Cohesion Policy

As one of the two most prominent components of public expenditure from the EU budget (along with support for agriculture), the performance of EU Cohesion policy has been at the heart of debates on the effectiveness of EU spending for almost two decades (Mendez et al. 2011; Begg et al. 2014; Polverari and Bachtler 2014). In the late 1990s, one of the two core structural policy goals of the Agenda 2000 reform package was to "improve the effectiveness of the structural policy instruments so that economic and social cohesion can be achieved" (European Commission 1997). The impact and added value of the Structural Funds were also central themes of the negotiations on Cohesion policy reform in the 2004–2005 period (Bachtler et al. 2013) at a time when the contribution of cohesion spending to EU growth was seen as mixed at best (Sapir 2003; Bachtler and Gorzelak 2007). Most recently, the need to improve the performance and results of Structural and Investment Funds were important motivations for the reforms introduced in 2013 (Berkowitz 2015; Bachtler and Mendez 2016). And, looking forward to the post-2020 period, the issue of effectiveness has already been highlighted by EU Commissioner for Regional and Urban Policy Corina Crețu, focusing specifically on the lack of convergence of many lagging regions despite (in the case of southern Europe) decades of EU and national support (Crețu 2015).

The continuing debate on the effectiveness of the policy is not due to a lack of research. Since the major reform of the Structural Funds in 1988, there has been considerable academic inquiry and extensive evaluation on the performance of Cohesion policy, more so than in any other area of EU expenditure (Polverari and Bachtler 2014). Yet one of the curious features of the policy is that there is surprisingly little consensus on how well it works, how effective it has been in reducing regional disparities and improving the performance of supported regional economies, and how useful it has been in fulfilling the goals set for it. Academic research and evaluation studies have reached widely differing conclusions on the results of interventions through Structural and Cohesion Funds.

There are many plausible explanations for this apparent paradox. A first is that the policy has had multiple goals that have, moreover, evolved substantially over time, making it hard to arrive at a simple assessment of cause and effect. In each programme period since 1989, the design of programmes has been subject to different strategic objectives at EU level and (in some cases) changing regional eligibility status, as well as different national or regional government priorities on the use of EU funding.

Second, Cohesion policy is only one among many influences on the transformations affecting regional economies, and many of the other influences will be more telling, especially where the scale of funding accruing to the region is moderate. This means that isolating the specific contribution of Cohesion policy, while theoretically possible using appropriate statistical techniques, is subject to pronounced uncertainty.

Third, regional transformation is a long-run process in which different determinants have to come together optimally to create cumulative effects that only happen after lengthy, and uncertain, lags. Minimum thresholds—for example, for connectivity or quality of basic services—may need to be attained before a favourable outcome becomes plausible. The quality of government and specifically the administrative capacity in managing authorities, implementing bodies and beneficiaries will also influence the effectiveness of resource allocation and project delivery.

Lastly, there have been formidable obstacles to evaluation. Until recently, there were no reliable comparable data on how Cohesion policy funds were spent under different programmes. Data for programme outcomes have often been unreliable or absent, and it has been difficult to establish relationships between EU spending and regional indicators for income, employment or other measures of economic development.

Against this background, the aim of this book is to investigate the main achievements of Cohesion policy programmes and projects, and their effectiveness and utility, over the long term from 1989 to 2012. It is the first study to examine the longitudinal performance of the funds for the entire period in which they have been available since the 1988 landmark reform, and to assess performance across regions from different EU countries. Focusing on the European Regional Development Fund (ERDF) and Cohesion Fund (CF), the study addressed three main questions:

• To what extent did the programmes address regional needs and problems over time?
• To what extent did the achievements of the ERDF and CF meet regional objectives in each programme period and across the entire period from 1989 to 2012?
• What are the main lessons learnt on the effectiveness and utility of ERDF interventions?

In analysing what the funds have achieved, the study looks at three dimensions of performance: the outcomes recorded by the programmes; whether these outcomes met the objectives set for them; and whether the outcomes succeeded in meeting the needs of the regions where the funding was spent.

The book is based on a research study, funded by the European Commission, which examined the achievements of all national and regional programmes co-financed by the ERDF and, where applicable, the Cohesion Fund in fifteen selected regions of the EU15 over the period from 1989 to 2012 (Bachtler et al. 2013) It therefore covered most of four separate programme periods—1989–1993, 1994–1999, 2000–2006 and 2007–2013.

Over these periods, regions were classified in various terms by the Commission depending on their level of development and hence need for funding. In the main, for the first three periods, regions were primarily classified as either Objective 1 regions with a GDP per capita of below 75 percent of the EU average, or Objective 2, which were above 75 percent of GDP but still experiencing development challenges such as high unemployment in old-industrial or rural regions. In the 2007–2013 period, a different classification was used of Convergence regions for the poorest (formerly Objective 1 regions) and Regional Competitiveness and Employment (RCE) for all other regions including those not formerly supported by the Structural Funds. In 2014–2020 yet another classification has been introduced: Less-Developed Regions, Transition Regions and More-Developed Regions.

Corresponding to this classification, the fifteen case studies were selected to cover three types of regions in ten countries (see table 1.1):

* *Less-developed regions:* regions eligible for Objective 1/Convergence support from 1989–1993 to 2012 (six regions);
* *Transitional regions:* regions eligible for Objective 1 or 6 at one time, but which subsequently were given Phasing-In/Out or Regional Competitiveness and Employment status (six regions); and
* *More-developed regions:* regions partially or wholly eligible for Objective 2/RCE status from 1989–1993 to 2012 (three regions).

The selection of regions was also influenced by three further criteria:

* scale of Cohesion policy support—regions with large programmes in a national context (based on regional EU funding as a proportion of member state allocations) with a bias towards member states that have been the largest recipients of EU funding;

Table 1.1. Case-study regions

Country	Objective 1/ Convergence	Phasing-In/Out	Objective 2/RCE
Austria		Burgenland	
Finland		Itä-Suomi	
France		Nord-Pas-de-Calais	Aquitaine
Germany	Sachsen-Anhalt		Nordrhein-Westfalen
Greece	Dytiki Ellada		
Ireland		Ireland	
Italy	Campania	Basilicata	
Portugal	Norte	Algarve	
Spain	Andalucía, Galicia		
United Kingdom			North East England

Note: further information on each of the regions is available at: http://ec.europa.eu/regional_policy/en/policy/evaluations/ec/2007-2013/#16.
Source: http://ec.europa.eu/regional_policy/en/policy/evaluations/ec/2007-2013/#16.

- geographical distribution—a 'balanced' representation of member states, as well as of different institutional contexts, in terms of domestic government arrangements, resource allocation systems and the role of domestic regional policies; and
- stability—in terms of regional administrative boundaries and (preferably) minimal changes in terms of institutional structures and management arrangements.

The geographical location of the fifteen regions is shown in figure 1.1. Collectively, these regions accounted for estimated EU spending of €146 billion over the period (see chapter 5).

The research in each region was undertaken according to a common, structured methodology involving five main elements. The study began

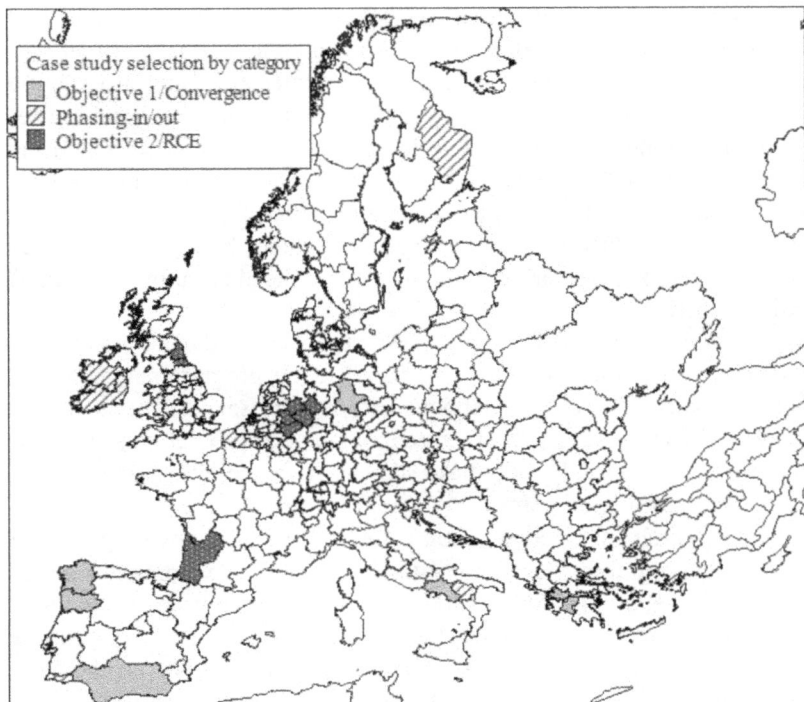

Figure 1.1. Case-study regions
Source: Project research.

with a *context analysis* of the initial regional development problems and needs at the outset of the period, the development paths in terms of regional GDP and unemployment, and the evolution of development needs over time.

Second, the research involved an analysis of the *evolution of strategies and expenditure* under each of the EU-funded programmes implemented in each region in each programme period. This included an assessment of the explicit strategies (as stated in programme documents) and implicit strategies (the rationale for spending decisions in reality), their relevance and synergies with domestic programmes. In the absence of published data on EU spending by programme (especially for the early programme periods) a unique database of expenditure was constructed.

Third, an analysis of *reported and actual achievements* was undertaken, comparing the indicators contained in programme reports with figures reported in other sources and taking account of the reliability of monitoring data. Fourth, the study involved an assessment of *achievements against objectives and needs*—the degree to which programme achievements met the objectives set at the start of a programme period (at programme and measure levels), and the extent to which the achievements met the needs of the regions according to various indicators. Lastly the research explored *the complementarities and synergies of the funding,* specifically the degree to which there was coherence across different EU interventions and with domestic (national/regional) policy priorities.

A central thread of the analysis was the use of 'thematic axes' (or themes) as a framework for understanding the programmes and their achievements. These were: innovation; enterprise; structural adjustment; infrastructure; environment; labour market; social cohesion and territorial cohesion. The themes were used for collating expenditure data and analysing outcomes.

The research involved secondary source research, covering a wide range of programme documentation (regional development plans, community strategic frameworks, single programming documents, operational programmes, annual implementation reports, programme final reports), monitoring data, ex ante, interim, ex post and thematic evaluation studies, national reports and academic research. In addition, a total of 543 interviews were undertaken across the fifteen regions with a wide range of respondents—government officials at national and regional levels responsible for regional development policy, programme-level strategy development and programming, and programme implementation, as well as external evaluators and academic researchers. These interviews were complemented by consultative workshops on the initial findings, bringing together a representative range of bodies and individuals. A large-scale online survey of organisations involved in programme or project implementation was also conducted in each region.[1]

This volume presents a concise, policy-orientated discussion of the findings and their implications for the future of Cohesion policy, drawing extensively on a synthesis report prepared for DG Regio and also available via its website at the same link as the case studies. For the most part, it does not seek to aggregate data or information on the results of programmes across periods or countries. The range of different sources used to reconstruct the evolution of programmes from 1989 to 2012, and in some instances (especially for earlier programmes) the questionable accuracy of some of the data, made this impossible. Instead, the book seeks to tell a story of how the resources invested through Cohesion policy were used, what they achieved in the different regions and the implications for research and policy practice.

The book is structured as follows. Following this introduction, chapters 2 and 3 discuss the theoretical and empirical approaches to the evaluation of Cohesion policy, and the innovative application of theory-based evaluation methods for this study. Chapter 4 reviews the evolution of the regional problem in the fifteen case-study regions, and the responses to those development problems through EU programme strategies are examined in chapter 5. In keeping with the theory-based approach to evaluation adopted, chapter 5 pays particular attention to the *implicit* strategies that often lay behind the declared objectives and the resource allocation choices made. Chapter 6 addresses the effectiveness of Cohesion policy interventions, that is, the degree to which stated objectives and targets were met, followed in chapter 7 by a discussion of the utility of achievements, that is, the degree to which policy results contributed to address the regions' needs. Chapter 8 reflects on the implications that the study has for the design and implementation of Cohesion policies and programmes. The book concludes with reflections on the lessons for the future of Cohesion policy after 2020.

Chapter One

NOTE

1. Further details on the methodology and full reports on the individual case studies are available here: http://ec.europa.eu/regional_policy/en/policy/evaluations/ec/2007-2013/#16.

Chapter Two

The Evaluation
of EU Cohesion Policy

EVALUATING STRUCTURAL AND COHESION FUNDS

Academic research and evaluation studies have reached widely differing conclusions on the results of interventions through Structural and Cohesion Funds. There are severe methodological problems associated with defining what would have happened in the absence of the policy—the counterfactual. For many of the regions that have been long-term recipients of funding from what are now known as the European Structural and Investment Funds (ESIF), the money they receive has become a core component of their public investment strategies, and it is not easy to define where they would otherwise be.

The academic and policy literature concerned with the evaluation of Cohesion policy is both very broad and very diverse. Studies come in many forms (academic papers, commissioned reports, consultancy projects, official evaluations, etc.) and employ many and diverse methodological approaches, reflecting the fact that there is no 'optimal' evaluation approach and that, rather, each method has its own strengths and weaknesses.[1] Three specific distinctions help in understanding the various approaches: the time of the evaluation; the scale or level at which the policy is being evaluated and the role of theory in the evaluation strategies.

A first distinction is between ex ante and ex post analyses. The former are often macroeconomic models of various kinds, of which the best known in the Cohesion policy context are HERMIN (Bradley et al.

2007; Bradley and Untiedt 2009) and QUEST (in t'Veld 2007; Varga and in t'Veld 2010). These seek to calibrate regional performance after shifting some policy parameters and evaluate the results against comparisons with outcomes in the absence of policy shifts—and depending on the model and time period, finding impacts on GDP of up to 6 percent. Other ex ante evaluations are rather linked more directly to qualitative research within the tradition of theory-based evaluation (TBE) and evidence-based policy (EBP). In this tradition, the policy intentions are analysed ex ante and juxtaposed against the policy means and instruments, taking into account the 'treated' context (e.g., the socio-economic, institutional, political, etc., environment of a recipient region or a beneficiary sector). The fit between these is then evaluated against past and parallel experiences, where outcomes have been evaluated as positive and where the impact of contextual factors (enabling or hindering these positive outcomes) has been successfully identified.[2]

Ex post analyses and evaluations have perhaps a broader range. They include macro-econometric studies examining the performance of target/'treated' groups (e.g., regions) controlling for a series of characteristics that are believed (usually, from theory) to affect the outcomes under study. A very common approach to evaluation (Davies 2014), these studies encompass research finding that Cohesion policy funding has had a positive and statistically significant effect on convergence (e.g., Becker et al. 2010; Mohl and Hagen 2010; Dall'erba 2005; Cappelen et al. 2003; Midelfart-Knarvik and Overman 2002), to those finding small or no effects (Hagen and Mohl 2008; Rodriguez-Pose and Fratesi 2004; Boldrin and Canova 2001). Ex post evaluations also include micro-econometric studies that often place more emphasis on identification issues and try to evaluate a 'treatment' against an empirically plausible 'counterfactual' (Bondonio and Martini 2012; Criscuolo et al. 2012; Hart and Bonner 2011; Trzciński 2011), again finding different effects on indicators such as employment, innovation on productivity.

Then there are qualitative analyses of programme outcomes, which themselves may be using a variety of approaches (including process-tracing, comparative case-analyses, in-depth studies of successes/failures) and methods (interviews, focus groups, participant observation, ethnographic research, etc.). There are also contextual/mixed-methods analyses, where descriptive data on performance are interpreted in light of more qualitative and contextual information, deriving from interviews with 'treated' recipients and policy officials (see Davies 2014).

Turning to the level of the evaluation, there is a spectrum covering those that assess the effects and effectiveness of the policy at large, those that concentrate on entire policy programmes (Ward et al. 2012; LSE et al. 2010; CSES 2003; ECOTEC 2003) and those that focus on the effectiveness of specific policy interventions/projects (e.g., CSIL and DKM 2012). Although it might be tempting to do so, it is difficult to derive a general proposition about which level of evaluation is the most appropriate. Successful policies are those that successfully implement *projects* that are relevant (i.e., addressing needs, offering utility) and produce tangible and identifiable results. In this sense, the crucial test for the success of a policy is on the logic, performance and outcomes of specific projects—which should then be the subjects of evaluation. On the other hand, specific interventions may have too limited a scope and their effects may be too nuanced to be successfully measured. A successful *policy* is one that manages to deliver on its overall objectives and to produce outcomes that are identifiable at the aggregate level. Put in more methodological terms, a focus on project evaluation may over-look crowding-out, deadweight and other effects (including opportunity costs, negative spillovers, etc.) that, on aggregate, may cancel out the positive outcomes of a particular intervention. Hence the focus should be on the aggregate intervention and performance.

By the same token, a focus on policy evaluation at large may in-troduce a lot of 'noise' (e.g., by conflating 'effort' with 'financial commitments', which is often an unavoidable compromise due to data limitations). This may lead evaluators to overlook outcomes that are much more 'localised' and 'nuanced', thus potentially arriving at erro-neous/invalid conclusions. From this perspective, the focus of analysis should be at a more disaggregated level. Generally speaking, studies at the aggregate level (policy evaluation) predominantly use quantitative techniques while analyses of specific projects tend to be more qualita-tive—with studies examining the effectiveness of programmes standing somewhere in the middle.

This partly influences (and is influenced by) the epistemological ap-proach taken in each of these type of studies. Analyses of projects (and programmes) are better suited, and actually seek, to identify the particular contextual and policy-related factors that determine success and failure of policy interventions. The concern is less with the measurement/ quantification of the size of the effects and more with the identification of the process and the particular conditions (including the 'intervening' and 'conditioning' variables) under which effects are generated. In contrast, aggregate policy analyses are geared towards the identification of general rules and patterns/trends. They seek to estimate, with an acceptable level of confidence (statistical or analytical), the average effect (and effectiveness) of a particular policy—thus allowing broader conclusions and discussions about cost-effectiveness, value-for-money and more widely the scope of the particular policy.

EVALUATION OPTIONS

As noted above, there is a wide body of econometric research assessing the causal impact of Cohesion policy on economic growth and regional convergence. This strand of the literature is mainly published in academic journals, rather than being commissioned as part of programme evaluations. The main analytical tool in this strand of research is some variant of the neoclassical growth model, that is, the production-function approach, specified either in strict neoclassical terms (constant returns to scale) or closer in line to the endogenous growth literature (i.e., incorporating increasing returns of some form). In this approach, economic growth (either output growth, labour productivity growth or total-factor productivity growth) is made a function of a number of input factors (labour, capital, raw materials, human capital, research and development, etc.—although not all of these are equally utilised, or controlled for, across studies), to which a Cohesion policy variable is added, most often in an ad hoc fashion (i.e., as an exogenous 'public investment' boost to aggregate output, but without hypothesising, and specifying theoretically, possible direct influences of Cohesion policy funds on the other factors of production).

The theoretical underpinning for this approach is the premise that Cohesion policy funding constitutes a form of 'public' investment that, like other forms of investment, raises the volume of (physical or human) capital of an economy and, plausibly, its productivity. This is a supply-side approach, where output is determined by the volume (and quality) of production inputs—rather than by demand, which in these models simply adjusts to supply through price changes. Demand-side models of the traditional Keynesian tradition, whereby Cohesion policy funds would act to stimulate aggregate demand and, through this, raise aggregate supply and productivity, are essentially absent from the econometric literature on the impact of Cohesion policy.

A wide range of econometric methods and techniques is employed in the literature, with varying degrees of sophistication (for a discussion, see Hagen and Mohl 2011). From an analytical perspective, many of these methods provide largely descriptive evidence, without much power to support causality claims. Other approaches, however, are better at controlling for endogeneity and causality, thus helping identify the nature and extent of the links between Cohesion policy spending and economic performance.

A shortcoming of this approach is that is sheds little light on the processes and mechanisms through which Cohesion policy has its effects—other than verifying or refuting the assumptions underlying the econometric specifications used and the economic models from which they derive. Another weakness is that these approaches rely on identifying 'average effects', even though the relatively small size of the policy (e.g., in relation to GDP or to other stimuli to growth) makes the potential effects difficult to capture.

A different approach to assessing the performance of Cohesion policy is to concentrate on the assessment of programme achievements in specific policy priorities, measures and actions, rather than on the impacts on aggregate macro variables of regional convergence or employment. To an extent, this approach has been driven by the European Commission's evaluation requirements and, contrary to the earlier approaches, has less visibility in the academic literature. Conceptually, the Commission's approach to monitoring and evaluation is underpinned by a 'logical framework' that assumes that the public funding (inputs) leads to a series of effects that can be split into outputs, results and impacts relating to different levels of programme objectives (European Commission 1999).

NOTES

1. In a way, this suggests that the different approaches should be regarded as complementary and thus evaluation efforts should seek to combine different approaches and methodologies through mixed-methods and triangulation.

2. See, for example, the study by Pawson and Kintrea (2002) on government subsidies in a domestic policy context.

Chapter Three

A Different Approach to Evaluating Cohesion Policy

Theory-Based Evaluation

Recent years have seen increasing attention paid to what is known as 'theory-based evaluation' (TBE). Drawing on the concepts of logic and utility, this approach encourages a shift from the assessment of formally stated objectives towards the mechanisms or theories of change underlying programmes and to the operationalisation of objectives that may not be explicitly or clearly defined. Although studies that explicitly or implicitly follow the TBE approach are not homogenous in their method, level of aggregation and focus, TBE's emphasis on process-tracing and theory-mapping justifies the aggregation of such studies into a distinctive category. As is discussed below, however, the application of this approach to the particular case of Cohesion policy is so far limited (Hart 2007); instead, examples are drawn from other studies on country-specific policy interventions with a regional or cohesion focus (Hart 2007; Kitching 2006; Mole et al. 2009).

The growing interest in the assessment of Cohesion policy programme logics—or 'theories of change' (Leuuw 2003, 2012; Barca 2009; Casavola 2009; Olejniczak 2009; Begg 2016)—is underlined in the Commission's monitoring and evaluation guidance for the 2014–2020 period. The rationale and key features have been summarised as follows:

> The importance of theory-based impact evaluations stems from the fact that a great deal of other information, besides quantifiable causal effect, is useful to policy makers to decide what policy to implement and to be accountable to citizens. The question of why a set of interventions

produces effects, how, for whom and under what conditions, intended as well as unintended, is as relevant, important, and equally challenging, if not more, than the 'made a difference' question. This approach does not mainly produce a quantified estimate of the impact, it produces a narrative. Theory-based evaluations can provide a precious and rare commodity, insights into why things work, or don't and under what circumstances. The main focus is not a counterfactual ('how things would have been without') rather a theory of change ('did things work as expected to produce the desired change'). The centrality of the theory of change justifies calling this approach theory-based impact evaluation. (European Commission 2011, 6)

The related concept of utility is starting to emerge as a more topical element in the framework of Cohesion policy evaluation. Whilst the word was included in the MEANS glossary already in 1999, little academic literature exists on this concept. The Evalsed source defines *utility* as "the fact that the impacts obtained by an intervention correspond to society's needs and to the socio-economic problems to be solved" (European Commission 2013a, 114). As Evalsed recognises, the notion "is a very particular evaluation criterion because it disregards all reference to stated objectives of an intervention" (ibid., 35). According to Evalsed, it is therefore especially meaningful in cases where objectives are not explicitly defined or are poorly defined, or when the evaluators expect a considerable amount of unforeseen effects.

THEORY-BASED EVALUATION

Central to this turn towards theory-based evaluation is the recognition of the need for assessment of programme achievements to be much more explicit about the regional development theories underpinning the rationale, causal mechanisms, relations and objectives of different forms of intervention. Although beyond the scope of this review, the theories that may inform theory-based evaluation are potentially wide-ranging and encompass various disciplinary and subdisciplinary perspectives (e.g., neoclassical economic theories, Keynesian theories, evolutionary theories of structural and temporal change, institutionalist political science theories, innovation and learning theories, endogenous growth theories, etc.) (Pike et al. 2011).

The focus of theory-based evaluation (as interpreted for the research in this book) is on understanding what it was that policymakers sought to change, and how policy action was expected to transform the region. The approach addresses the logic behind the policy interventions, whether such logic was appropriate for regional circumstances and how policy evolved as initial needs were met and new ones had to be confronted.

The concept of utility has particular resonance in the context of the long time span of Cohesion policy interventions examined in this volume. Political priorities and circumstances have changed in the course of the two decades covered by the research, and to assess the longer-term impact of evolving Cohesion policy programmes requires taking a step back from the changing programme goals and assessing the achievements of the ERDF in the selected regions from a 'fixed' viewpoint, that is, goals that can be considered as 'sensible'/relevant today. Yet this entails an ex post reassessment of what the programme's goals should have been. This is a task that requires the research team to be aware of methodological and ethical challenges: the risk that the team imposes *their* understanding of what the ERDF should deliver and of the very role of public policy in economic and social development, which are clearly politically charged issues, and the risk of confusing utility as it would be perceived today with utility as interpreted at the time of the intervention.

A key consideration shaping the methodology is that the purpose of the study is to investigate the impact of programmes implemented under Cohesion policy and not to assess regional performance as such. The distinction is critical because the objective is to establish whether policy interventions addressed the right issues for the region and achieved what they set out to do. Overall regional performance is, ultimately, what interests citizens and decision-makers alike, but will not always be the best test of whether programmes achieve what is expected of them.

Instead, the primary purpose of the study is to understand what led to change and thus to focus on causality rather than on whether the outcomes are 'better' than the counterfactual of what would have happened in the absence of the policy interventions. Thus, the core of the research is to investigate why and how policy had effects, and to develop narratives about the role of policy in shaping regional performance. It follows that, although there is inevitably an interest in whether regions benefiting from ERDF support have improved their performance, the purpose of the evaluation is not to disentangle the contribution of policy relative to the many other determinants of regional change. Hence what is expected of the approach is that it can establish whether interventions led to the effects and achievements that theory would predict.

The essence of TBE is to start by identifying the rationale for policy interventions and then to assess whether the outputs from these interventions result in outcomes for society that are as intended. The first stage requires information on what the logic of intervention was, but it entails going beyond what might have been written down in planning documents. Instead, the focus should be on elucidating the model of development or conceptual framework in the minds of the programme architects. Second, the evaluation has to investigate empirically whether the policy interventions achieved what was intended. Piecing together these elements of the approach, the test of whether policy is effective will be whether its outcomes flow from the policy itself or are the result of exogenous factors.

An immediate difficulty concerning TBE is that the design of programmes is a complex process influenced by multiple demands and by a wide range of stakeholders who have their own preferences for the approaches that should be adopted. In these circumstances, it is improbable that there will be a single neat theory that sums up the intervention logic. Often, too, programmes will be drafted in a way that (perhaps deliberately) obfuscates the true aims of the exercise in an attempt to forestall opposition. Thus, the explicit programme logic and objectives, formulated in programme documents, may differ from the implicit objectives revealed in how resource allocation decisions are made in practice.

TBE can also focus on different stages of a process of change and, by so doing, can make it easier to separate how the intervention caused change to occur (Mayne 2011). In this way, it will be easier to ascertain how interventions made a difference, thereby opening the 'black-box'.

For this ambitious study, the methodology is necessarily complex. It brings together qualitative and quantitative methods, and it has to be sufficiently flexible to accommodate different theoretical and conceptual models, the shifting expectations and goals of Cohesion policy, an evolving institutional framework and data limitations. This section sets out the overall methodological approach and explains how the different components of work feed into the research strategy.

Because the study covered policy interventions spanning up to a quarter of a century, there were unavoidable problems in obtaining robust and consistent information, especially for earlier programming periods. It is also important to stress that the lens through which Cohesion policy is viewed has changed over time. For this reason, the interpretation of needs, objectives and achievements has to be cautious: what made sense at the time may no longer look persuasive. Equally, applying contemporary evaluation criteria can result in a distorted view of the effectiveness of past policy. Therefore, the methodology sought to bring out these complications and to afford room for different judgements on the effectiveness of Cohesion policy in different regions at different times and over the period as a whole.

THE LOGIC OF INTERVENTION

The concept of the *logic of intervention* is vital to understanding the rationale for policy interventions, whether the logic was appropriate for regional circumstances, and how policy evolved as initial needs were met and new ones had to be confronted. The approach recognises that regional development theories have themselves evolved over the period studied, as has the wider context in which Cohesion policy is implemented, notably because of major EU strategies such as Lisbon/Europe 2020 (Nordregio 2009; Begg 2010; Mendez 2011).

In the early years of the period under study, enhancement of infrastructure was regarded as a necessary condition for regional development and was a favoured policy, especially in many lagging regions (see, for example, Biehl 1991; de la Fuente and Vives 1995; Bachtler and Gorzelak 2007). The logic behind these interventions was that unless regions had sufficient levels of physical capital, they would be systematically disadvantaged in comparison with more developed competitor regions, not least in attracting inward investment. Human capital investment and efforts to promote enterprise were also typical of this era; many national regional policies during the 1960s, 1970s and 1980s were based on various forms of regional investment and employment aid to disadvantaged regions to compensate for the higher costs of less desirable locations for productive investment (Bachtler 2001).

The 1990s saw a profound shift in thinking and practice in regional development policies at national and EU levels with the emergence of a new conceptual basis, different policy goals and changing implementation arrangements. By the end of the 1990s, underlying theories of regional development were paying increasing attention to sources of endogenous growth, with innovation and research-led economic development stressed in policy packages, and a focus on entrepreneurship, productivity and other aspects of 'competitiveness'. Regional policy shifted from focusing on selected 'problem regions' to investing in all regions, with increasing decentralisation of policy implementation to regions, more investment in the business environment and soft infrastructure, and a greater use of evaluation in more countries (Amin and Tomaney 1995; Storper 1995; Malecki 1997; Morgan 1997; Cheshire and Magrini 2000; Bachtler 2001; Rodriguez-Pose 2001).

These trends intensified and spread to more countries during the 2000s, driven by a more prescriptive approach to economic development by the EU, through the Lisbon agenda. To varying degrees, greater prominence was given to social cohesion as a determinant of economic growth, to sustainability issues in the design and delivery of interventions, and to community-based development especially in urban areas. The latter part of the decade was marked by the effects of the economic crisis, which saw much greater attention being given to national competitiveness and sectoral policies (Bachtler and Davies 2010) as well as regional resilience (Bristow 2010; Davies 2011). It was also characterised by global and European debates about spatially blind versus place-based policies (World Bank 2009; Barca 2009; OECD 2009) and the role of institutions in explaining variations in economic growth and development (Farole et al. 2010; Rodriguez-Pose 2013).

As programming approaches in Cohesion policy and intervention logics have evolved over time, the information available to appraise them has also become more structured and systematic. This is particularly true of statements of programme objectives and of the manner in which the achievements of programmes are articulated. Possibly the most basic sense of achievement is simply spending the budget, with little or no regard to whether doing so had tangible effects on well-being. A somewhat more refined sense of achievement is whether or not targets were met, for instance, for kilometres of road or levels of skills attained. But often what was really intended in programmes was not clearly stated, and as a result, assessment of achievements is likely to be incomplete. From a TBE perspective, what matters is whether the assumptions and logic behind a programme are shown to have been justified; in this sense, what matters is whether the implementation of the programme led to the results that its architects sought and anticipated.

Looking at different regions over different time periods is expected to reveal a wide range of intervention logics and, as a consequence, will provide tests of a variety of 'theories' of regional development or 'narratives of change'. Two likely findings—the first often revealed by TBEs, according to Weiss (1997)—are that many of the approaches will have been tacit rather than explicitly stated in strategies and that the theories will evolve over time even where the needs being addressed are long-term.

RESEARCH CONCEPTS

Investigating the logic of intervention to understand effectiveness requires clear-cut definitions of key concepts. At the core of this research are the concepts of achievements, relevance, effectiveness and utility, respectively defined as follows.

Achievements are defined as the outcomes of interventions, including those that are directly linked to specific interventions as well as the broader contribution of programmes (individually and jointly considered) to wider societal objectives, recognising that such objectives are likely to evolve over time. They include outcomes that might not have been originally planned, but that nevertheless affect well-being. Critically, this notion of achievement calls for an understanding of why the policy intervention made a difference and thus whether or not the logic of intervention was well conceived. In looking at policy achievements over the long term, cumulative achievements are of central importance. It is important to stress that this conceptualisation of achievements will not always be reflected in regional performance and should not be confused with the latter.

Reported achievements are understood as the outcomes (outputs, results) and impacts reported by programme monitoring systems and reporting tools, and by evaluation studies and other research, which may be different from the achievements effectively realised. They may include progress towards meeting the targets set in programme strategies. An aim of the study has been to ascertain whether these results and impacts embraced prospective outcomes that correspond to broader objectives.

Relevance is the 'appropriateness of the explicit objectives of an intervention, with regard to the socio-economic problems the intervention is meant to solve'. This concept concerns whether the programme strategies, goals and priorities were sufficiently attuned to the needs of the regions, and whether the balance of expenditure and effort was well judged to meet these needs (European Commission 2013a, 110). Relevance is therefore a concept to be employed in assessing the policy structure and internal coherence of programmes.

Effectiveness is understood as the extent to which programmes achieved the goals stated. This entails two distinct types of goals: on the one hand, the outcomes specified in the programmes; on the other hand, the wider changes that were intended to occur as a result of the policy intervention, or in other words the contribution (impact) expected from the intervention (European Commission 2013a, 110).[1] These two types of effectiveness require different methodological approaches, which are described in detail below.

Utility is interpreted as the extent to which programmes led to impacts that are in line with 'society's needs and to the socio-economic problems to be solved', which may differ from the goals explicitly stated in the programmes themselves or which may not have been stated explicitly in the programmes. This requires a reassessment of the needs that the programmes should have addressed, a task that was carried out with a mix of quantitative and qualitative methodologies. As discussed in chapter 7, the concept of utility is particularly useful where objectives are not explicitly defined or are poorly defined, or when unforeseen effects are anticipated.

The methodological approach to assessing relevance, effectiveness and utility of Cohesion policy was based on bottom-up empirical research in each of the case-study regions. This began with an assessment of the regional development context (problems and needs) and a programme analysis—involving a review of the strategies employed and the expenditure associated with these strategies—which allowed an assessment of the relevance of strategies in relation to needs. Achievements were examined using a range of sources by programme period and then across each of the eight thematic axes. This was used to analyse overall effectiveness of interventions at programme and measure levels and across all fifteen regions. The utility of Cohesion policy support was assessed in both qualitative and quantitative terms, enabling an assessment of the legacy of the funds in each of the fifteen regions. Lastly, the research findings from each of the case studies and comparative research across all fifteen regions were used to draw conclusions on the achievements of Cohesion policy and lessons for the future of the policy.

NOTE

1. Also see DG Regio (2011).

Chapter Four

What Was the Problem?

Regional Development Challenges and Needs

Understanding the achievements of Cohesion policy must start with an assessment of the development challenges and needs of the regions assisted and how these needs evolved over time. The chapter reviews the regional development problems and needs of the fifteen case-study regions in the late 1980s, grouping the problems under the headings of major underdevelopment, sparsity and peripherality, industrial decline and restructuring, and spatial and labour market disequilibria. The chapter then examines the development paths of the regions according to GDP per head and unemployment over the period from 1989 to 2008. Growth performance is analysed according to a framework introduced by Camagni (1991a, 1991b) and developed by Affuso et al. (2011), which identifies six patterns of regional growth; initial needs and their evolution are discussed according to these six patterns. Further insights are provided through a qualitative assessment of the evolution of regional needs under the eight thematic axes that are used throughout the study as a framework for evaluation.

INITIAL REGIONAL DEVELOPMENT PROBLEMS AND NEEDS

At the start of the study period (late 1980s), all the case-study regions were relatively disadvantaged, as befits recipients of ERDF funding. They had significantly lower levels of development, as measured by GDP per capita, for example, whether relative to their national averages (e.g., North East England), relative to the EU average (e.g., Dytiki Ellada) or both. In the late 1980s, GDP per capita, measured in constant 2000 prices, ranged from less than €10,000 in the case-study regions of Spain (Andalucía, Galicia), Portugal (Algarve, Norte) and Greece (Dytiki Ellada) to near or above €20,000 in Nordrhein-Westfalen, North East England and Aquitaine—against an average EU15 GDP per head in 1989 of €17,239 (according to Cambridge Econometrics data). The principal explanation for these differences is the relative prosperity of the respective member states, and these national differences mean that there is a degree of heterogeneity among the regions—both those initially designated as Objective 1 and those designated as Objective 2 in 1988.

The nature of needs and the main economic-development problems facing these regions varied greatly. There were differences in fundamentals, such as accessibility and the quality of various forms of infrastructure, in industrial composition/specialisation, as well as in the relative performances of national economies. Partly for the last reason, the regions differed significantly in terms of the vibrancy of their labour market. Unemployment rates were significantly higher—and well above the national and European averages—in deindustrialising North East England, in remote and sparsely populated Itä-Suomi, and in the more agricultural economy of Andalucía. However, they were significantly lower (and closer to national averages) in regions such as Burgenland, Dytiki Ellada, Algarve and Norte. In some regions, unemployment (and employment loss) had started to become a more pressing issue because of long-term structural shifts. This was the case in Sachsen-Anhalt (because of the post-communist transition), Basilicata (because of falling agricultural employment) and Campania (which underperformed relative to the national average because of weak industrial development, but where the unemployment rate may have been overstated because of the size of the shadow economy). Although less pronounced, a rise in unemployment associated with structural change in the economy also characterised the two case-study regions of France (especially Nord-Pas-de-Calais).

Despite having, broadly speaking, similar initial conditions of relative underdevelopment (as measured by GDP per head) and/or unemployment, the case-study regions represented a broad range of structural characteristics and associated needs. Drawing together the analyses undertaken, four main groups of problems and sets of development needs can be identified among the three groups of regions investigated:

a. major underdevelopment characterised by shortfalls across all indicators;
b. sparsity of population and peripherality (either geographical or in terms of connectivity), with the two often going together;
c. a generally weak economic base, manifested in an over-specialisation in declining traditional heavy industries, agriculture or other low value-added traditional activities, coupled with an underrepresentation in high-growth, higher value-added sectors; and
d. the presence of disequilibria in regional economies, such as problems of skill mismatch (typically due to deindustrialisation) or of inactivity and weak labour supply, or spatial disequilibria such as between urbanised coastlines and rural interiors.

Many of the regions exhibited more than one sort of problem or development need with, for example, interactions between weak connectivity and declining industries (Basilicata) or between the decline of a traditional industrial base, skills mismatch, environmental problems and weak entrepreneurship (Nord-Pas-de-Calais). Some regions such as Campania, Andalucía or Norte fit into all four groups. In this sense, needs cumulated to constitute multiple disadvantages. Hence the distinctions are less a typology of regions as such, but more an identification of the dimensions on which each of the regions can be assessed.

The most fundamental challenges were faced by regions characterised by major underdevelopment associated with disadvantages ranging from a lack of basic infrastructure and services, to deficits in skills, often compounded by peripherality (national or European) or significant internal disparities. These regions experienced needs across almost all of the eight thematic axes, though sometimes in a different way from other classes of region. For example, they tended to have an entrepreneurial sector consisting largely of small and micro businesses that were traditional in nature, but also lacked connections to large companies or to external networks.

Regions had to make tough decisions about which needs were to be prioritised, often with the added constraint of conforming to Structural

Funds' regulations and navigating multiple operational programmes with objectives that could be difficult to reconcile. Inconsistent or incompatible domestic economic development policies also created complications. Prioritisation would also usually have consequences for the internal disparities or disequilibria due to the difficulty of raising performance on several thematic axes across the whole region simultaneously. A particularly hard choice lay in deciding between providing general social and infrastructure development across the whole region, and a focus on industrial development that could require agglomeration in selected urban centres or (for example, in Campania) choosing between development models targeted at large or small firms.

For regions with relatively low population densities, weak urban agglomerations (for some), rurality and depopulation, transport and connectivity were major challenges. They also had a need to develop new models of development able to boost employment opportunities (especially in rural areas), often through tourism, but also through the development of localised centres for industry and services.

Problems of rurality, accessibility and population sparsity are facts of life and not readily amenable to immediate policy action, and it is unsurprising that regions with these characteristics have often struggled to reverse the demographic trends or resolve problems of connectivity. Moreover, the very long-term nature of the investment need has to be taken into account, as major projects may need to span two or more programme periods in Cohesion policy, as was shown by the various stages of developing the Rion-Antirion Bridge in Dytiki Ellada.

The regions subject to industrial decline and restructuring faced a range of restructuring difficulties, depending on their past specialisations and economic trajectories. Industrial decline and the associated restructuring problems reflected skills mismatch in the labour market and, eventually, inactivity and structural unemployment. For the regions transitioning from traditional industry or centrally planned economies, the needs tended to be more focused around economic transformation (enterprise, innovation, skills) and the consequences of restructuring in terms of derelict land and replacing outdated infrastructure. Social needs were usually a secondary issue and consisted more of how to deal with the consequences of deindustrialisation (pockets of high unemployment) rather than widespread needs for hospitals and schools. The central issues were halting decline and rebuilding employment, and converting the often-polluted sites of old industry (e.g., mines and steelworks) for new industries and incubators.

For these regions, outcomes improved faster in cases where the public sector took a more active role in addressing problems of industrial decline, lack of diversification and unemployment (e.g., North East England). Spatial imbalances or disequilibria in the labour market were particularly pressing in 1989 in some of the deindustrialising regions of the 'north' and in some of the more traditional, but relatively more developed, economies of the 'south'. Spatial imbalances were addressed not only through transport infrastructure investment, but also through industrial restructuring (for instance by encouraging supply chains between the more traditional and the more dynamic/high-tech segments of the local economies), economic diversification measures (such as support for tourism in rural areas), social infrastructure (nurseries, schools, hospitals) and regeneration of town centres. For some regions, industrial restructuring led to the emergence of supply side pressures and skill shortages (Galicia and Andalucía) or chronic skills mismatch (Nord-Pas-de-Calais).

ECONOMIC PERFORMANCE AND NEEDS

There is no easy link between the initial status of a region and its subsequent performance. Analysis of the evolution of GDP per head and unemployment rates for the fifteen regions relative to national trends and for the group as a whole is provided for each region in Bachtler et al. (2013). Given the diversity of the regions examined, and the corresponding performances and needs, as well as the long time frame of the analysis, it is difficult to establish a general trend or classification. Although analysis of the comparative evolution of the case-study regions reveals a notable degree of mobility, regional evolutions appear to be neither linear (e.g., towards general improvement) nor universal (in the sense of applying similarly to all regions). To the extent that a general pattern can be identified, it is that regional evolution has largely followed the wider national trends.

By definition, the regions classed in 2007–2013 as Phasing-In/Out manifestly achieved more than some of their counterparts, because from similar starting points they had grown sufficiently to exit Objective 1 status by the mid-2000s. Yet as the most recent data show, these gains proved to be vulnerable to the crisis. The relationship between growth performance and other indicators was surprisingly varied. Where economic growth was driven much more by gains in labour productivity than in employment (Sachsen-Anhalt), the wide-ranging restructuring was accompanied by a sharp increase in unemployment.

Further insights into the dynamics of output and employment growth can be gleaned by examining changes over time relative to the EU average. Patterns of employment and productivity growth can be shown in a single chart[1] by plotting productivity growth against employment growth. This decomposition can reveal whether change in the economy stems from productivity gains arising from new and efficient firms or by the 'dropping off' of inefficient production.

This approach presents productivity and employment change relative to the EU27 over the period from 1991 to 2008 (see figure 4.1). A region may develop at the same rate as the EU Gross Value-Added (GVA) either if both productivity and employment grow at the same rate as the EU average, or if productivity increases at a lower rate, but employment does so at a proportionally higher-than-average rate, and vice versa. This is shown by the diagonal line. If a region is above this line, it increases its total GVA more than the EU27 average; if it is below the line, the GVA growth rate is below average.

The performance of the fifteen regions is assessed here over the majority of the study period. Analysis of performance in each of the programme periods can give quite varied results as some regions grew more rapidly in one period rather than another (see Bachtler et al. 2013, 10).

Figure 4.1 indicates that most of the regions performed worse than the EU average in growth of GVA over the period (that is, they lie below the diagonal line), although their distribution across the graph indicates different patterns of regional economic development. Plainly, there is no straightforward inference to be drawn about the three categories of regions studied. Phasing-In/Out regions are to be found on both sides of both the dimensions of the chart, while the three RCE regions are close to the centre of the chart, albeit a little below. Aquitaine, which is more rural (with a preponderance of Objective 5b funding, that is for rural development, during the 1990s), does better than the other two RCE regions with regard to employment growth. Among the group of

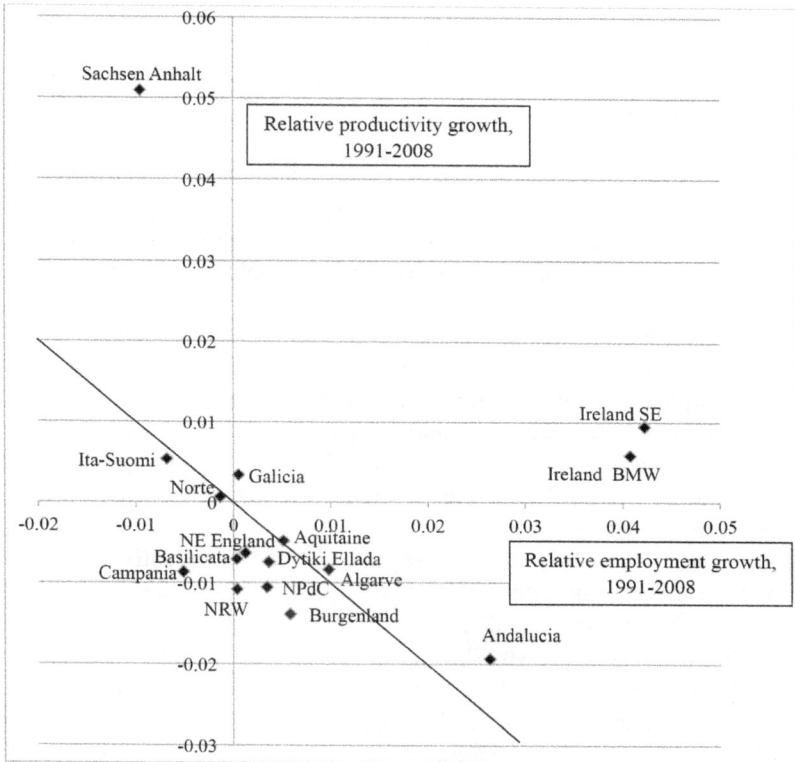

Figure 4.1. Relative productivity and employment growth, 1991–2008
Note: NRW = Nordrhein-Westfalen. NPdC = Nord-Pas-de-Calais.
Source: Cambridge Econometrics and Eurostat data. Figure produced using method developed by Camagni (1991a, 1991b) and refined by Affuso et al. (2011).

Convergence regions, Andalucía stands out for its employment growth while Sachsen-Anhalt is the major exception to the underperformance in productivity for most of the others in this group.

In this chart there are six analytically distinct segments, depending on whether the region is located above or below the EU average for each of the two main axes, and above or below the diagonal line. This gives rise to a terminology, developed by Affuso et al. (2011), which can be used to classify the development paths of the regions. The findings for the fifteen regions are as follows. Seven of the case-study regions lay above the diagonal line of EU average productivity and employment performance, in segments termed 'virtuous cycle', 'economic take-off' and 'restructuring'.

- *Virtuous cycle* is used to describe a regional economy that exceeds EU average growth as a result of higher-than-average growth of both productivity and employment. In the period under review, which was before the onset of the sovereign debt crisis, only Ireland, which succeeded in exiting Objective 1 status, was able to show a consistently good performance in the virtuous cycle segment, with growth in both employment and productivity, although with a bigger emphasis on employment. Both Irish regions (Border, Midland and Western; and Southern and Eastern) are shown here, and both performed similarly well. Galicia lies just inside this segment with a small average relative growth in productivity, but little relative growth in employment.
- *Economic take-off* is when lower-than-average productivity performance is offset by very good employment performance, so that the effect on total value added is positive. Andalucía and the Algarve both show GVA growth slightly above the EU average and strong employment growth despite a reduction in relative productivity. As neighbours, albeit in different groups for the purposes of this study, they share some common features. In these regions, a rapid expansion of employment explains overall output growth, but the expansion has been in sectors that are performing worse than the EU average, and the evidence in both cases suggests that growth was driven by tourism. Aquitaine also has modest employment growth but a slightly better performance on productivity.
- *Restructuring*, when higher-than-average productivity growth is associated with declining employment, leads nevertheless to good GVA performance due to the increases in productivity. Sachsen-Anhalt was the only region of the fifteen in the restructuring segment, illustrating its dramatic increase in productivity alongside employment loss, suggesting new higher-value activities as well as a reduction in low-value sectors. Although classed as an Objective 1 region, the specific circumstances of the transition in eastern Germany probably outweigh the direct influence of Cohesion policy.

This leaves the other regions underperforming the EU in categories termed 'dropping out', 'relative decline',[2] and 'industrial conservatism'.

- *Dropping-out* is when productivity growth is achieved alongside lower-than-average employment growth usually by the closure of inefficient production units, where the cutting of low-productivity activities results in higher-than-average GVA growth. Itä-Suomi and Norte have recorded a relative reduction in employment as old declining sectors were closed down, leaving a relative growth in productivity. Again these findings transcend the specific group to which they are allocated for the present study.
- *Industrial conservatism* is when poor productivity growth is accompanied (and sometimes explained) by better-than-average employment growth, a pattern that is more likely to take place in the presence of public assistance and industrial rescues. Six regions fall into this segment—North East England, Nordrhein-Westfalen, Basilicata (all close to the borderline with the 'relative decline' segment), Nord-Pas-de-Calais, Burgenland and Dytiki Ellada—meaning that although they have increased employment, it has been accompanied by lower-than-average productivity growth, suggesting that growth has been in low-productivity sectors, perhaps supported by interventions. The fact that there are respresentatives of all three groups of regions in this category signals that how a region is designated for Cohesion policy purposes may be of limited value as a predictor of its performance.
- *Relative decline* is defined as a vicious cycle in which both productivity and employment perform worse than the average and even the rationalisation of employment does not restore competitiveness. Only one region performed poorly on both productivity and employment (Campania) and appears to be locked into this vicious cycle of relative decline, although an argument might be made about special circumstances associated with flawed implementation of Cohesion policy, rather than this being a reflection of Objective 1/Convergence status.

This analysis is, however, limited to the period up to 2008 and the onset of the economic crisis. Since then, some of these regions have seen dramatic reductions in GVA and employment, giving a different set of results that illustrates the short-term effects of the crisis rather than the evolution of regional performance through the study period. The analysis shown here portrays how the regions performed over a period of relatively strong growth.

Drawing the analysis of regional needs together, a summary overview of the main needs of each region at the beginning of the study period, and their evolution in relation to the eight thematic axes outlined earlier, is presented in figures 4.2a and 4.2b. The table indicates how

	Infrastructure		Distribution of econ. activity/ spatial disparities		Labour market & human capital				RD&I
	Basic infrastructure essential services	Peripherality / external accessibility	Internal connectivity	Internal disparities	High unemployment and/or hidden economy	Long-term unemployment	Weak education levels	Lack of specialist skills	Weak private sector R&D
Sachsen-Anhalt	Major*	Major	Major		Major	Worsened			Worsened
Dytiki Ellada	Major	Limited	Major		Major		Major		
Campania							Limited		
Norte	Major						Major		Major
Andalucía	Major	Limited*			Major				
Galicia	Major*	Limited*	Major						
Burgenland	*1			Limited				Major	
Itä-Suomi									
Nord P. de Calais							Limited	Major	
Ireland	Major	Major			Major	Major		Major	Major
Basilicata	Major	Limited					Major		
Algarve		Major							Limited
Aquitaine		Limited	Major		Limited				
NR-Westfalen					Limited				
N.E. England		Major			Major	Major			

Key: ▨ Major improvement (* needs largely met)   ▦ Limited improvement

▪ Situation has worsened

Notes: (1) Refers only to water supply and waste water infrastructure. (2) Ruhrgebiet only.
Source: Project research – analysis by Vassilis Monasteriotis.

Figure 4.2a. Evolution of regional needs: 1989–2012 (from 1991/1995 for later accession countries/regions)

	Enterprise				Structural adjustment		Social inclusion		Enviro sustainability
	Weak industrial base	Dominance of micro and small firms	Weak entrepreneurship culture	Low productivity	Modernisation of primary sector	De-comm./recovery of old industries	Social exclusion/poverty	Out/immigration/ ageing / commuting	Environmental problems
Sachsen-Anhalt			▦	▨		▨	■	▦	▨
Dytiki Ellada	▦		■			▨			
Campania		▦					▦	▦	
Norte		▦		▦	▨				
Andalucía			▨	▦					▨
Galicia			▨	▨	▨	▨			▨
Burgenland	▨				▨				
Itä-Suomi				▦					
N.P de Calais						▦		▦	▨
Ireland	▨			▨				▨	
Basilicata		▦					■		
Algarve	▦				▨				■
Aquitaine					▨				
NR-Westfalen				▨		▦			
N.E. England				▦		▨			▨

Key: ▨ Major improvement (*needs largely met)   ▦ Limited improvement   ■ Situation has worsened

Notes: (1) Refers only to water supply and waste water infrastructure. (2) Ruhrgebiet only.
Source: Project research - analysis by Vassilis Monasteriotis.

Figure 4.2b. Evolution of regional needs: 1989–2012 (from 1991/1995 for later accession countries/regions)—continued

different areas of need are perceived to have changed over the period from when they first qualified for Cohesion policy funding in 1989.[3]

The areas in which most improvement has been made are in the provision of basic infrastructure and essential public services as well as internal and external connectivity. This applies to all the regions where development needs were greatest and is what would be expected for Objective 1/Convergence regions.

For other development needs, the picture is more mixed. Ireland is adjudged to have made the most progress in meeting a broad set of development needs, and a wide range of needs has been addressed at least to some extent in several others. Dealing with enterprise-related development needs seems to have been most difficult across all regions, particularly weaknesses in entrepreneurial culture and encouraging the growth of small- and medium-sized enterprises (SMEs). The same applies to research, development and innovation (RDI), where little progress appears to have been made in all fifteen regions in promoting more private RDI investment. The table suggests that some development needs have intensified in certain regions, especially in Sachsen-Anhalt (notwithstanding the progress made with restructuring noted above) with respect to long-term unemployment, RDI investment and some aspects of social exclusion.

These patterns reflect important and persistent differences among the regions in terms of structural characteristics and corresponding needs. Convergence regions typically experienced underdevelopment across all thematic axes, whereas problems tended to be more narrowly concentrated in regions facing industrial decline. Most regions faced internal disparities, presenting particular challenges for the prioritisation of actions. Notwithstanding similarities in initial needs, the regions experienced different journeys over the study period, reflecting a combination of national development trends and regional policy choices.

NOTES

1. This approach was introduced by Camagni (1991a, 1991b) for manufacturing and extended to the whole regional economy by Affuso et al. (2011). Relative employment growth is on the horizontal axis, and relative productivity growth is on the vertical axis. A 135° negatively sloped line passing through the origin denotes regional GVA growth equal to the average. For this analysis, productivity and employment data were used for the period from 1991 to 2008. The 1991 data rather than 1989 were used as the starting point, as the 1989 data were not available for one of the regions, and 2008 was used as the end point rather than 2010, which was the most recent year available at the time of the study, as the 2009 data showed dramatic drops in most of the regions as a result of the global financial crisis, and hence the final year would have a dramatic and in some respects a highly distorting impact on the overall trend.

2. In this context, it may be preferable to revise the definition used in Affuso et al. (1991), who called this segment 'deindustrialisation'.

3. The table is based on qualitative assessments undertaken in the case-study research. In representing the evolution of needs, the table does not make inferences in relation to the causal factors that might have driven the described change and, in particular, on whether the change is to be attributed to the intervention of Cohesion policy or other policy interventions. Also, the problems and weaknesses listed are often interrelated.

Chapter Five

Regional Strategies and Their Relevance to Needs

In analysing how EU programmes responded to regional development needs and challenges, the study examined the evolution of strategies and expenditure under each of the EU-funded programmes implemented in each region in each programme period. As noted earlier, this included an assessment of the explicit strategies (as stated in programme documents) and implicit strategies (the rationale for spending decisions in reality), their relevance and synergies with domestic programmes. In the absence of published data on EU spending by programme (especially for the early programme periods), a unique database of expenditure was constructed in order to assess where and how funding was actually committed. Interview research with a range of stakeholders involved in programme design, and with external commentators, provided further insights into the motivation of those developing the regional development strategies.

THE ROLE OF A STRATEGY IN EU PROGRAMMES

In order to receive ERDF support, each of the regions in the study was required to develop multi-annual programmes to identify interventions that addressed the perceived needs of the region. The nature of these programmes varied over time and, to varying degrees, there were multiple programmes for any one period, sometimes with a strategic framework document such as a Community Support Framework or (for 2007–2013) a National Strategic Reference Framework.

A strategy can mean many different things, sometimes several different things simultaneously. At a simple level, it is a narrative associated with an individual plan, setting out objectives and how they will be achieved. This may be quite mechanistic as a formal planning statement where the steps towards a desired outcome are set out as a blueprint for specific policy actions. Alternatively, the strategy may be a loose framework indicating directions within which a range of participants can develop their own strategies and where the final strategy emerges from a process of experimentation and reflection. Or it may be used to set out a vision and set of common objectives and implementing arrangements, providing a unifying framework for a range of organisations. Regions typically pursue a spectrum of such strategies, often interacting in ways that can make it difficult to establish what the most important objectives are and the order in which they are to be achieved.

At one level, a strategy might concern the mix of measures and interventions and how these relate to the objectives to be achieved: this is what is usually considered as the programme strategy. However, regions typically obtained support from multiple programmes, so that another level of strategy relates to how the region integrated these various programmes, and what their relationship was with any wider regional development strategy. In the latter interpretation, an overarching strategy may identify what is to be done across a variety of programmes, and may specify the contributions to be made by individual programmes. It may, though, be less prescriptive and could be limited, for example, to how much funding is allocated to different areas of public expenditure.

Where there are multiple strategy documents, plans or programmes at different levels of governance, these may be in different forms. For example, a programme focused on infrastructure might have a planning style of strategy in which the actions are specified precisely at the outset in terms of the roads or railways to be constructed against a particular timetable, whilst a programme for business support may have very much looser aims and objectives. In the latter case, it may be that the actual strategy itself evolves over the course of the programme and is, therefore, subject to considerable flexibility.

A related issue is the potential for both explicit and implicit strategies. Each Structural Funds programme approach had a written strategy that stated explicitly what was to be done. However, the organisations implementing programmes may, individually or collectively, have had their own goals for economic development, which may have differed from these explicit strategies, and may not be formally recorded. Such implicit strategies may influence the use of the funds in ways that lead to divergence from the explicit strategies. This is more likely where regions have underlying aims and objectives that differ from the guidance provided for the Structural Funds; for instance, where the Commission has proposed minimum levels of expenditure around particular objectives.

Further, implicit strategies different to those spelt out in programme documents may emerge during implementation, as a result of a process of adapting programmes to meet practical constraints and unplanned difficulties. A seven-year time frame is relatively long in public policy terms. Reflecting this, Structural Funds regulations acknowledge the possibility of shifting resources between areas of spending, modifying the relative weight of instruments implemented, and introducing new instruments or refining criteria for selecting projects (with latitudes and modalities that can be changed from one programme period to another). These changes to the content of programmes, which may be introduced without altering the description of programme goals or priorities, mean that the strategies actually pursued may become markedly different to those formally stated, but without explicit recognition of this.

It follows from this discussion that regional strategies are likely to be complex and often contested, with different national and regional bodies prioritising different objectives according to their competences and responsibilities, and also with potential differences between national and regional bodies, as well as between the rationales behind national and regional programmes. A final overarching question is whether the region has an underlying development strategy, likely to be implicit, which drives the strategies of the individual programmes, or whether the Cohesion policy strategies in the region drive regional strategies. In the latter case, especially if wider EU imperatives such as the Lisbon/ Europe 2020 strategies map out key policy orientations for which the ERDF is seen as an instrument, national and regional governments may need to develop regional strategies where they did not previously exist. In some cases, these top-down pressures require institutional adaptation because the regional scale of policy was not previously recognised.

THE RELEVANCE OF EU
PROGRAMME STRATEGIES 1989–2012

The research revealed major differences in the relevance of strategies across regions and over time. Some of the fifteen case-study regions had a clear vision of how they wanted to use the resources from the Structural Funds in at least some periods, most obviously those in which a single regional operational programme (OP) was closely linked with a collective regional strategy. Others had multiple ERDF programmes at national and regional levels being implemented in the region, alongside other domestic spending programmes. In these regions, an overall regional strategy, even for the Structural Funds, could only be inferred from implicit assumptions about suitable responses to regional need and future development opportunities. There were national-level overarching strategies for the coordination of programmes, notably the Community Strategic Frameworks (CSFs) in earlier periods and, more recently, the National Strategic Reference Frameworks (NSRFs) covering all regions within the same country, irrespective of Cohesion policy status; however, these did not always comprise clear and visible strategies for individual regions. Consequently, it is unsurprising that the fifteen regions were polarised between those with a single, dominant and holistic strategy for the ERDF programme and regions with multiple and complex overlapping programmes in which holistic strategies were lacking or were much less evident.

Furthermore, strategies evolved over the period since 1989–2012 with changes in policy and eligibility, learning effects and domestic governance structures. Sometimes these changes led to a clarification of strategies and greater coherence, although not in all cases, as some developments added to the confusion.

The regions initially characterised by major underdevelopment and deficits on all indicators—notably the Objective 1/Convergence regions as well as Ireland, Basilicata and Algarve (all of which were classified as Objective 1 at the beginning of the study period)—were in countries in which the structure of support initially involved national ERDF programmes with varying degrees of regional-specific programmes. National operational programmes were usually driven by the investment strategies of government departments, for example, in the development of national transport and communications networks, and they were only weakly connected at either national or regional level. These national programmes then often failed to integrate with what were sometimes weak regional operational programmes. The weakness of distinct regional voices in strategies in most of these regions meant that their national and regional programmes diverged considerably.

In the early programme periods, Italian regions had been accustomed to receiving most of their support through many national multiregion operational programmes (MOPs) as 'baskets' for the allocation of expenditure, without an overarching underlying theory or relationship with the regional operational programmes (ROPs). The situation only improved in the late 1990s when, in parallel with wider national-level developments, which saw more weight being placed on economic theories as a basis for policy design, these regions gradually developed their own abilities to draft regional development strategies. However, Basilicata is an example of a region that, at least during the first two programme periods covered, had a comparatively clear vision for how it wanted to develop, based on a comprehensive Regional Development Plan that had initially been prepared during the 1980s. As regions also mainly lacked separate domestic regional strategies, the consequence was a series of parallel programmes with their own internal logic but poorly connected to each other. Over time, however, strategies became less fragmented and more regionally specific.

In some countries the structure of support initially involved national ERDF programmes with varying degrees of regional-specific programmes. Portugal and Greece, for instance, had no tradition of regional-level government, and regional strategies were essentially driven by national policy objectives. National acceptance of the role of the Algarve as the main tourism region nevertheless meant that it was incorporated into programme strategies. Ireland, prior to 2000, was distinctive among the fifteen case studies through having only national programmes integrated into a National Development Plan, with no separate regional ERDF programmes. Leaving aside the Irish case, the regions typically struggled to adopt coherent strategies across the many programmes at national and regional levels, with in some cases relatively weak capacity at the regional scale to develop complex strategies.

There were sometimes differences between the explicit strategies as stated in programme documents and what regions were really trying to achieve, or what might be called 'implicit strategies'. However, the explicit and implicit strategies tended to become more aligned in later programme periods. Where strategies reflected objective analyses and ex ante evaluations from the start, as in Ireland, this helped to ensure that they were clearly formulated and implemented in line with objectives. They also commanded a reasonable degree of political consensus and within the different branches of the state administration (with some exceptions in relation to specific themes).

For most of the fifteen regions, however, the strategies set out in programme documents during the 1990s tended to be general, mono-thematic or generic, lacking evaluation evidence and sound needs analyses. This tendency, which was by no means a peculiarity of the case-study regions (see, for example, the review of Objective 2 strategies in Bachtler and Taylor 1999), had two main implications. First, the explicit strategies could hide a reality of diverse interests and assumptions on the part of stakeholders. In Algarve, for example, the programmes were underpinned by an implicit assumption that tourism would increase through investments in transport and environmental infrastructure, although this was not stated clearly in the programmes. In Nord-Pas-de-Calais, in the first two periods, the explicit focus on reconversion/transition hid a continued preference for supporting traditional sectors, which were an important source of employment and had a strong symbolic value for workers and local authorities (particularly in 1989–1993). Local authorities in many regions were also a favoured beneficiary of ERDF spending because of domestic financial constraints.

Second, the limited sophistication of early strategies also meant that the explicit strategies could be open to interpretation, leaving extensive scope for flexibility during implementation, and sometimes leading to discrepancies between the explicit strategy and what was actually pursued. As an example, in Aquitaine, the divergence between explicit and implicit strategies up to 2006 was because regional-level managing authorities were unable to dictate what local authorities did. Thus, support to urban areas was implemented mainly through the redevelopment of public spaces rather than the other forms of support foreseen by the programme, such as social and cultural innovation. The generality of explicit strategies was not necessarily due to inexperience or lack of capacity: in Itä-Suomi it was a strategy in itself. The general objectives, in successive programmes, were attributable to the difficulty of having to accommodate four quite different NUTS 3 subregional strategies, which inhibited the setting of specific goals and targets for the region as a whole.

Few strategies were clearly underpinned by specific theories of economic development, although instances can be found of a nod towards endogenous development in the 2000–2006 period in Basilicata and Campania or toward regional innovation systems in North East England. Attempts to reconstruct ex post the underlying theories, as part of the case-study research, indicated multifaceted, muddled and contradictory development models. In fairness, however, the strategies were often drawn up according to the prevailing domestic or EU economic thinking of the time, such as the view in the late 1980s and early 1990s that (for Objective 1 regions) infrastructure development was a main source of economic growth, and similarly in later periods, cluster policies began to be introduced in line with the emerging academic evidence.

For the most part, the regional objectives were remarkably stable over time, tending to evolve incrementally rather than being radically overhauled at the beginning of each programme period (a trend that was also true in other EU regions—see Bachtler et al. 2000 and Taylor et al. 2004). The new orientation of the EU Community Strategic Guidelines in 2007 emphasised innovation, and often tallied with domestic paradigm shifts within the regions. In Nordrhein-Westfalen, for instance, the 2007–2013 programme entailed a fundamental shift in objectives, whereby support for structural adjustment and employment was superseded by competitiveness and adaptability, and the territorial focus on the Ruhrgebiet was discontinued. Similarly, in Nord-Pas-de-Calais, there was a clear shift towards Lisbon priorities for the 2007–2013 programme, which represented a fundamental change in direction. Although ostensibly driven by EU requirements, it was also embedded in the framework of domestic policies, notably the competitiveness poles and the new 'regional innovation strategy', elaborated with the support of the European Commission and aligned with the *Contrat de Projet Etat-Région* and the Regional Economic Development Scheme (SRDE 2005).

Overall, the perception among programme authorities, other stakeholders and external experts was that programmes had improved over time. They had also become more specific, measurable, attainable, relevant and timely (SMART) in terms of the expectations of the European

Commission. However, they varied in their success in this respect, and in some cases there were reversals.

Taking the SMART attributes in turn, programme objectives are expected to be *specific*, clear and unambiguous. However, there was a tendency in many of the programmes to have general statements about improving development in the region and unrealistic ambitions of closing the gap with national or EU averages, without specific objectives that connected with the needs of the region. Many programmes were generic, and could have been adopted in other regions. Whilst strategies did become more regionally specific over time, there was also some convergence due to the pressure from the Commission to address EU-wide Lisbon objectives.[1]

Considerable progress was made in making objectives *measurable*, although more needed to be done to meet expectations for the 2014–2020 period.[2] During the 1990s, programmes lacked quantified targets and monitoring systems. Later programmes often had some form of impact measure, but the metrics used were frequently crude and poor measures of the interventions. This led to projects seeking to optimise the measurements rather than delivering the best results for the region. In addition, some objectives were not easily amenable to quantified targets, and were best described in qualitative terms, although this presented problems for measurement and estimating whether the project was as successful as it should have been, given the resources invested.

Some of the programme-level objectives were overambitious, and hence not *attainable*. Setting a target for an activity needed a detailed understanding of how that target would be achieved. This could be relatively simple for a construction activity where relative costs were known, but much more difficult in interventions where benchmarked costs were unknown, or where activities were highly heterogeneous and the mix was not known in advance. Even for construction, though, there were often problems of poor targets being set, one explanation being that assumptions about costs were shown to be unreasonable. Missed targets in many regions could be attributed to poor implementation, but also to unrealistic targets.

The *relevance* of programmes was a central issue in the study, examined in more detail below. The crucial question was whether programmes were designed to meet the real needs of the region. As noted above, many of the regions saw some fragmentation of interests as different stakeholders had different conceptions of the needs of the region. Thus, if the needs were contested, then there would inevitably be disagreements about what was relevant.

Finally, objectives are expected to be *timely*, with a realistic timescale over which objectives should be achieved with the resources available. This was automatically introduced in some respects by the nature of programmes that set a specific timescale for interventions, although they usually did not specify the timescale over which results were expected—especially where the scale of ambition was much greater than could be achieved within the programme period. This then introduced problems of evaluation, especially where results arose only after (and sometimes, long after) the programme ended. In most regions, this was due to inadequate consideration of the time frame over which interventions could be assessed. Major infrastructure projects exemplified the difficulty because many required support from successive programmes.

EXPENDITURE PATTERNS AND TRENDS

Analysing trends in spending of Structural and Cohesion Funds over time and across regions has always been problematic. Multiple sources, inconsistent reporting, and delays in closing programmes and finalising expenditure have presented major challenges for comparative research. It is only in the 2007–2013 period that the European Commission was able to introduce a structured, systematic approach to member states reporting on the financial progress of programmes. This study, therefore, has had to undertake primary research based on a bottom-up classification and aggregation of measure-level expenditure information, undertaken for each of the fifteen regions, according to the methodology described in more detail in Bachtler et al. (2013). Notwithstanding important data limitations and gaps, this is the first analysis of long-term expenditure trends for the entire period from 1989 to 2012, reconstructing ex post the final expenditure at NUTS 2 level.[3]

This section reviews the expenditure patterns and trends across the fifteen case-study regions. It begins with an overview of total recorded spending, and then discusses expenditure trends by thematic axis and category of regions.

Overall Expenditure Trends

Over the period from 1989 to 2012, more than €146 billion of Structural Funds are estimated to have been spent in the fifteen regions (see figure 5.1). The Objective 1/Convergence regions had the largest share, of 68.3 percent (c. €99.6 billion), with Phasing-In/Out and Objective 2/RCE regions representing a more modest 21.6 percent (c. €31.5 billion) and 10.1 percent (c. €14.7 billion), respectively. Across the entire period, allocations exceeded expenditure by around €14 billion (c. 9 percent of the initial allocation). This figure should, however, be interpreted with great caution, given that, especially for early periods, it was not always possible to reconstruct the non-earmarked regional allocations of the national or multiregional OPs (which overinflates expenditure compared to allocations) and that this sum is negatively affected by the expenditure delays of the 2007–2013 programmes.

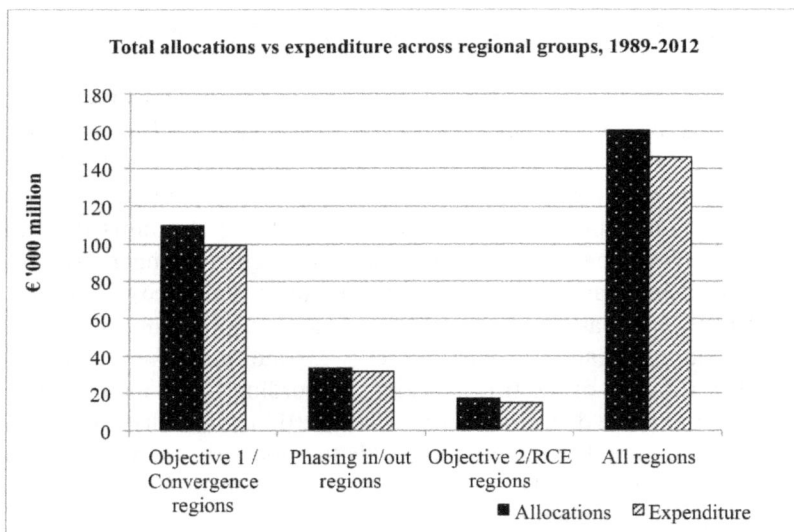

Figure 5.1. Total Structural Funds allocations compared to actual expenditure by regional groups and across all fifteen regions (1989–2012)—'000 million euro, 2000 values

Source: Data included are for ROPs and, where applicable, NOPs combined. There are some data gaps in relation to the early periods and MOP/NOP expenditure, which could not always be regionalised. Details can be found in the case-study reports at: http://ec.europa.eu/regional_policy/en/policy/evaluations/ec/2007-2013.

The discrepancy between planned and actual expenditure is the highest in absolute terms in the Objective 1/Convergence regions (c. €10.2 billion). Again, however, the lack of reliable data on allocations for some of the MOPs/NOPs affects the validity of this funding.

Expenditure by Thematic Axis

Turning to the analysis of expenditure by thematic axis, figure 5.2 shows the total Structural Funds expenditure of each region across the whole study period, 1989–2012, and the relative weight assigned to the eight thematic axes. Andalucía and Norte spent the most (with c. €26.3 and €29.9 billion, respectively), followed closely by Sachsen-Anhalt (€20.4 billion) and Campania (€17.5 billion).[4] Burgenland is the region with the lowest spending, c. €1.7 billion over the entire period: not a negligible figure nevertheless, given the size of the region and the fact that Cohesion policy support started only in 1995, and in GDP terms

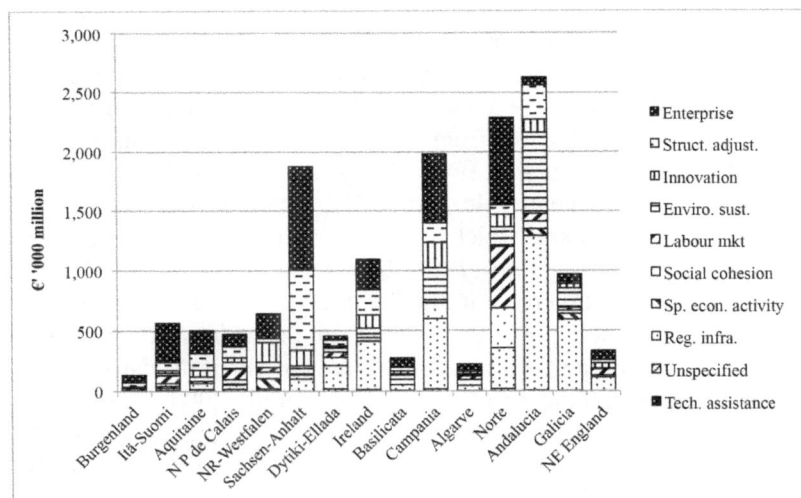

Figure 5.2.   Total Structural Funds expenditure per region and theme—'000 million euro, 2000 values
Source: Data included are for ROPs and, where applicable, NOPs combined. There are some data gaps in relation to the early periods and MOP/NOP expenditure, which could not always be regionalised. Detail can be found in the case-study reports at: http://ec.europa.eu/regional_policy/en/policy/evaluations/ec/2007-2013.

(representing c. 3.78 and 2.32 percent of GDP in the 1995–1999 and 2000–2006 programme periods).

The proportion of spending across the themes varies considerably among the regions, ranging from a strong emphasis on enterprise support in Burgenland (56 percent of total expenditure from 1989 to 2012) and Itä-Suomi (59 percent), to a predominance of infrastructure spending in the two Spanish regions (representing 61 percent of total expenditure in Galicia and 49 percent in Andalucía), in Dytiki Ellada (43 percent), and in Ireland (37 percent). Aquitaine, Sachsen-Anhalt and Campania show a concentration of expenditure on two main themes (enterprise and structural adjustment in Aquitaine and Sachsen-Anhalt, and enterprise and infrastructure in Campania), whilst the remaining regions display more mixed expenditure patterns, with no dominant theme.

The relative distribution of expenditure across the eight themes and its evolution over time can be more precisely appraised from the next three figures, which provide a period-by-period disaggregation of expenditure for the three regional aggregates, for (in turn) the Objective 1/Convergence regions (figure 5.3), Phasing-In/Out regions (figure 5.4) and Objective 2/RCE regions (figure 5.5).

Figure 5.3 shows a predominance of infrastructure spending across all programme periods (except 2007–2013) in the Objective 1/Convergence regions, ranging from 43 percent of total expenditure in 1989–1993, to 27 percent in 1994–1999 and 30 percent in 2000–2006, and to a low of 14 percent in 2007–2013. Another prominent theme is structural adjustment, which remained over 20 percent from 1989 to 1999 (22 percent in 1989–1984, 24 percent in 1994–1999) but decreased sharply to 6 percent in the 2000–2006 period before growing again to 13 percent in 2007–2013. The main thematic shift across periods in this group of regions was the relative growth of the categories of social cohesion and labour markets starting in the 2000–2006 period. Perhaps surprisingly, innovation is shown as remaining broadly stable, accounting for 5 and 10 percent of total expenditure in the first two programme periods, and then 7 percent in 2000–2006 and 8 percent in 2007–2013. The environmental theme too remained broadly stable throughout, at around 15 percent of total expenditure, with a downward trend in 2007–2013 (11 percent, compared to 12–17 percent, respectively, in previous periods).

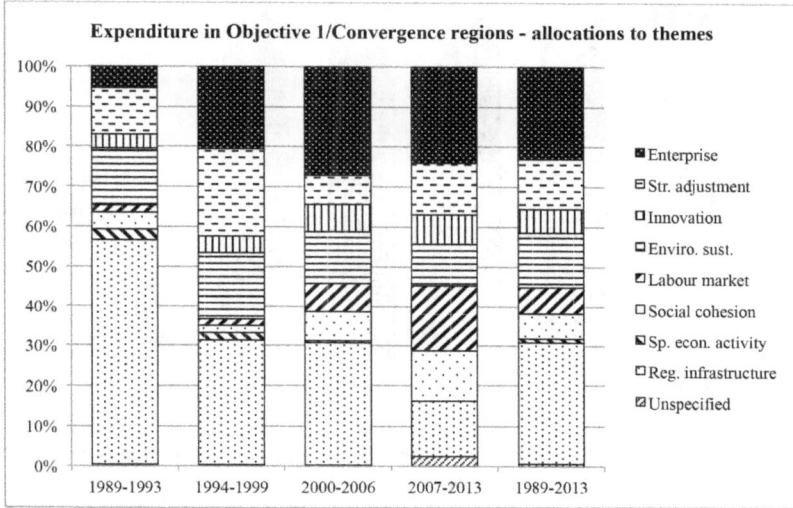

Figure 5.3. **Structural Funds expenditure in 'Objective 1/Convergence' re-gions—percentage allocations to themes by programme period**
Source: Data included are for ROPs and, where applicable, NOPs combined. There are some data gaps in relation to the early periods and MOP/NOP expenditure, which could not always be re-gionalised. Detail can be found in the case-study reports at: http://ec.europa.eu/regional_policy/en/policy/evaluations/ec/2007-2013.

The situation is similar in the 1989–1993 period for the Phasing-In/Out regions (figure 5.4), with expenditure strongly polarised around infrastructure (58 percent of expenditure). However, the composition of expenditure in Phasing-In/Out regions becomes more diversified over the following programme periods, with a predominance of enterprise support (34 percent, 38 percent and 21 percent, respectively, in 1994–1999, 2000–2006 and 2007–2013) and, in the 2007–2013 period, structural adjustment and innovation (respectively at 23 and 22 percent of expenditure).

Lastly, figure 5.5 demonstrates a strong focus in the three Objective 2/RCE regions on enterprise in the first three programme periods (with 50 percent of the money spent on this theme in 1989–1993, later fall-ing to 30 percent [1994–1999], 35 percent [2000–2006] and 14 percent [2007–2013]) and a marked shift towards innovation and social cohe-sion in the current period. In the 2007–2013 period, moreover, there

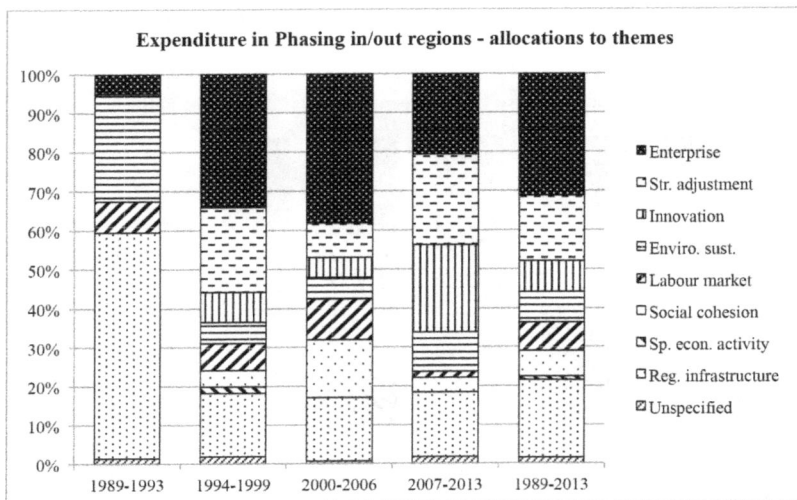

Figure 5.4. Structural Funds expenditure in 'Phasing-In/Out' regions—percentage allocations to themes by programme period

Source: Data included are for ROPs and, where applicable, NOPs combined. There are some data gaps in relation to the early periods and MOP/NOP expenditure, which could not always be regionalised. Detail can be found in the case-study reports at: http://ec.europa.eu/regional_policy/en/policy/evaluations/ec/2007-2013.

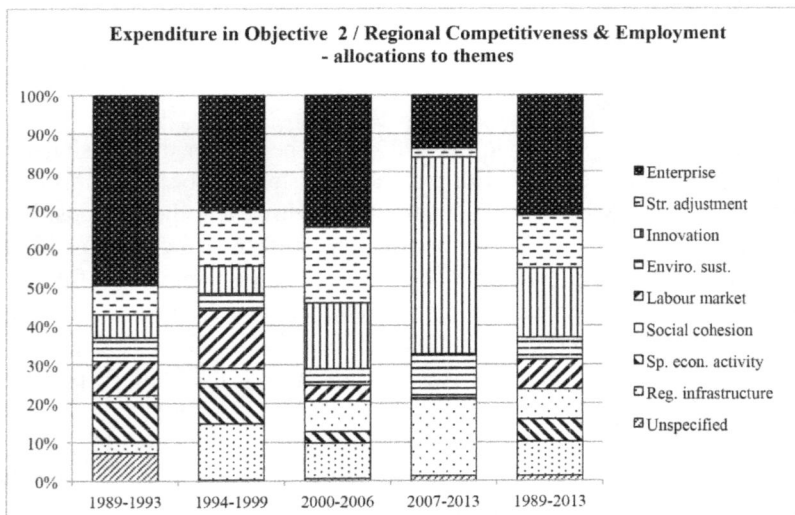

Figure 5.5. Structural Funds expenditure in Objective 2/RCE regions—percentage allocations to themes by programme period

Source: Data included are for ROPs and, where applicable, NOPs combined. There are some data gaps in relation to the early periods and MOP/NOP expenditure, which could not always be regionalised. Detail can be found in the case-study reports at: http://ec.europa.eu/regional_policy/en/policy/evaluations/ec/2007-2013.

is no expenditure on labour market measures in this group of regions, largely due to the mono-fund nature of the programmes. In the Objective 2/RCE regions, two themes record the least expenditure throughout the study period: spatial distribution of economic activities and environmental sustainability. However, whilst the former has progressively diminished (from 10 percent in both 1989–1993 and 1994–1999, to 3 percent in the 2000–2006 period and no expenditure in 2007–2013), the latter has seen its share double since 2000–2006 (from 4 percent to 11 percent of total expenditure).

NOTES

1. A source of weakness in the development of specific objectives, which is also relevant for the 2007–2013 generation of programmes, was the unpreparedness of regional administrations at the time. In this regard, the fifteen regions were not an exception. A recent study by DG Regio on twenty-three pilot managing authorities in fifteen member states found that programme objectives tended to be generic, and that the logic of intervention in programmes was often weak, with priorities often resulting from the aggregation of 'more or less related' subpriorities. The study underlines that some programmes 'were designed in a deliberately vague fashion so that resources could be spread thematically and geographically' (European Commission 2013b, 9).

2. Inaccurate target setting is also not a problem exclusive to the fifteen regions covered by this study. The European Commission in its working document on the 2013 Strategic Report found that even in 2007–2013 programmes, 'target setting remains perhaps the most widespread and substantial problem. In a number of cases, targets were not set. Where targets were set, many were often substantially over- or underachieved' (European Commission 2013c, 21).

3. The ex post evaluations of the 1994–1999 ERDF programmes, for instance, only include reflections on commitments (ECOTEC 2003; CSES 2003); the synthesis report of the ex post evaluation of 2000–2006 ERDF programmes includes elaborations on non-final expenditure data (at 31 December 2008), at member state level only (Applica et al. 2009), whilst the thematic study on 2000–2006 ERDF and Cohesion Fund regional expenditure, undertaken when the programmes were still underway and published in 2008, whilst focusing on subnational data (NUTS 2 and NUTS 3), only provides information on commitments (SWECO 2008). The report produced by the DG Regio Evaluation Network on the 2007–2013 programmes (Ciffolilli et al. 2013) provides the thematic breakdown of the programmes' planned, rather than actual, expenditure. In relation to expenditure, the report focuses mainly on its evolution and on the reprogramming shifts between categories (i.e., planned expenditure).

4. The data limitations already noted apply. In particular, the figures for Basilicata are underestimated given that the data included in the analysis only comprise ERDF (and not all Structural Funds) and the ROPs only for the 1989–1993 and 1994–1999 periods. Similarly, for Algarve and Dytiki Ellada, actual expenditure is underestimated by the lack of data on the expenditure for some or most of the NOPs.

Chapter Six

The Effectiveness of Programmes in Achieving Objectives

The considerable investments made by the ERDF in the fifteen case-study regions, as shown in the previous expenditure analysis, can be expected to have made significant differences to the development of these regions. Increasingly, these expectations have been specified in the objectives of programmes as noted previously, and this chapter examines the nature of the achievements in the regions as a result of this investment.

MEASURING ACHIEVEMENTS

There is no simple, single assessment of achievements: they can and have been assessed over time in a variety of different ways, sometimes rigorously, sometimes barely at all. This chapter begins by reviewing the nature of achievements and the methodology used in assessing reported and actual achievements. As noted earlier, the study distinguishes between two sorts of achievements.

- *Reported achievements* are as reported by the programme managers in their annual and final implementation reports to the European Commission. Typically, these are output measures reflecting the activities undertaken by projects, indicators relating to the effects that the projects have on beneficiaries and the wider region, and qualitative case studies of projects and their results.

• *Actual achievements* may differ from those reported because the latter may underestimate or overestimate achievements, for a number of reasons explained in the next section. The calculation of actual achievements at programme level requires either detailed auditing of each project or macroeconomic analysis. An assessment of actual achievements is made on a thematic basis to identify what kinds of interventions have worked in each of the regions.

ERDF expenditure in any region will deliver various types of achievements. They encompass the direct outputs of the projects and the wider changes they stimulate within the region; they can be anticipated by formal targets or can be unanticipated or accidental; they can be measured using numerical metrics or softer indicators, or be purely qualitative in nature; and they can have positive or negative consequences for the region. The complex nature of achievements presents problems for research and evaluation, as some things are measurable and measured, whilst others are not. A comprehensive view needs to cover all aspects, but usable data are inevitably easier to obtain for the measured aspects, even if what is measured may not be the most useful indicator of desired changes.

A second level of reported achievements is results and impacts. During the programme periods covered in the research, managing authorities were advised by European Commission guidance to define *results* as the (immediate) effects on the direct beneficiaries of the actions financed, while *impacts* were the longer-term effects of interventions on the global or specific objectives of the programme. Impacts were typically reduced to a small set of indicators such as employment created, increase in SME activity, or a more thematically specific indicator, such as numbers of new firms created. Outputs may be the direct and sole result of an intervention—a project to build a road will result in kilometres of road built—but impacts are more likely to be the consequence of a combination of ERDF intervention and other activities. As an illustration, a new firm may be partly assisted by an ERDF project, but it will also be the result of additional private investment and, possibly, nationally funded interventions as well.

Despite the emphasis placed by programme reports on the development of quantitative measures of outputs, they only tell part of the story, even though ever-more-complex metrics have been developed to capture the diverse forms of interventions, such as advice to firms. Sensible output indicators for activities such as business support are difficult to identify—differentiating between advice given in a seminar or over the phone, and an intensive consulting engagement can be made by referring to the time or cost involved, but does not necessarily reflect the quality of the advice. Aggregation across a range of projects then becomes impossible. Instead, some achievements are best identified through qualitative targets and descriptions of services offered. The assessment of quantitative reported achievements by programme managers faced a number of difficulties that may have led to under- or over-reporting, not least because programme managers usually depend on projects to provide data. Managers of projects, in turn, may have limited information on some kinds of outputs, may find it difficult to attribute the outputs of projects to standard indicators, or may provide misleading information to programme managers.

The process of aggregation also potentially introduces errors where double-counting occurs. There may be several projects aiming to provide advice to firms, each reporting the number of firms assisted. In some cases, this approaches the number of firms in the region as each incidence of advice is counted separately, even though the indicator might be the number of firms assisted. Recognising that there is multiple counting here, it is still impossible to know whether a large number of firms received some advice or a small number of firms each received many different interventions.

THE REPORTED ACHIEVEMENTS OF EU PROGRAMMES

The scope for measuring achievements convincingly has grown over the years as the EU institutions have become more demanding in their information requirements, reflecting demands for enhanced accountability. In the 1989–1993 period, the requirements for reporting achievements were almost nonexistent, and most regions did little more than to demonstrate that funding had been spent on the projects that had been agreed on. The indicators that were available related to either financial progress or physical output indicators, such as kilometres of roads built, and in some, lists of projects were produced (e.g., Campania).

The 1994–1999 period saw more detailed development of indicators and targets, of both outputs and results. However, this was not done systematically across all regions, although overall, regions reported a wide range of outputs. There were also inconsistent approaches to measurement of key variables. In some regions, estimates of jobs created were limited to the regional programmes only, or even to specific measures, implying relatively few jobs generated, even though many more may be created through national infrastructure programmes or business support programmes that cover the region. The missing data render comparisons with total regional employment or expenditure misleading, with the result that the impact on the local economy may be badly underestimated.

The 2000–2006 programmes were much more oriented to the Lisbon agenda, and hence they had a greater focus on enterprise and innovation, reflected in targets for outputs and results. The 2000–2006 programmes saw further efforts to enhance monitoring processes, and more specific output and results indicators, but output indicators were still diverse and were sometimes too numerous to be accurately tracked. With substantially larger budgets in many regions and a greater emphasis on support for firms, the jobs-created estimates tend to be much higher than the previous period, although doubts remain about their accuracy. As an illustration, Andalucía reported a figure of 317,000 jobs as being 'safeguarded' by the programme; apart from the contentious concept of jobs 'safeguarded', this appears to be a generous estimate, although it should be noted that some 780,000 jobs were created in the region between 2000 and 2006 according to Eurostat data, taking total employment to 3.1 million.

At the time of the study, data for the 2007–2013 period were limited due to delays in launching many programmes, the lags in the production of annual implementation reports and the effects of the reorientation of programmes to fit new challenges and situations. Although there were modest improvements in the specification and implementation of output target indicators and greater attention paid to economic results, there were still problems in monitoring the achievements of ERDF programmes. In some regions, such as Andalucía and Galicia, new information systems were introduced but with delays in their operationalisation. Some regions have been reducing the number of indicators. Itä-Suomi, for example, both reduced the number of indicators and defined them more precisely, removing the indicator for 'renewed jobs' and refining the definitions of the remaining employment figures.

To arrive at a better understanding of the longer-term achievement of the programmes, the research for the study analysed the achievements under the headings of the eight thematic axes noted earlier. In each region, the outputs of activity related to each theme were reviewed alongside additional evaluation information and interviews with beneficiaries, programme managers and other stakeholders. The aim was to understand the detailed nature of interventions within each theme, how they related to objectives and needs, what the underlying theories that led to intervention choices were, and what changes happened as a consequence.

Innovation

Investment in innovation had grown in significance over the 1989–2012 period from being a very minor priority in 1989–1993 to one of the largest components of spending in some regions in 2007–2013 (see figures 5.3, 5.4 and 5.5). Achievements in this area increased dramatically over time, as well as often shifting in emphasis as regions gained experience of intervention in support of research and technological development (RTD) and innovation, and developed more sophisticated approaches to regional innovation systems. In a number of regions, the initial focus was on building up public research capacity, mainly in universities, with a gradual broadening out of the agenda to encompass business R&D, innovation support and science parks. Elsewhere, the initial focus was on accommodation for innovative business with a shift to include investments in research and innovation networks, or on stimulating R&D growth, especially after 2000, to meet the target (a headline one of the Lisbon and Europe 2020 strategies) of 3 percent of GDP being spent on R&D. Often, this was led by investment in the public sector, and especially universities, which could most easily absorb the investment.

Such approaches have undoubtedly been beneficial in boosting the overall level of research in some of the regions, although the degree of sustainability varies. Ireland used ERDF to build up research institutes to underpin key sectors of the economy and modernised the universities as a core element of a knowledge-based economic development strategy. In Portugal and Spain, the considerable funding that went into research projects in universities lacked such a strategic vision, and the long-term benefits are more dubious. A lack of prioritisation, with funding being distributed widely across large numbers of research groups, also seems to have been less effective in translating into economic development. Nevertheless, a presumed result of this investment across all Spanish regions was a doubling of Spanish contributions to global scientific publications, from 1.28 percent in 1990 to 2.63 percent in 2004, with Andalucía slightly increasing its share from 13.1 to 14.4 percent of the increased level of Spanish publications.

In the private sector, firms were supported through technology transfer offices in the universities and a smaller number of private-sector projects, but the achievements were uneven. A notable success is the Technology Park of Andalucía, which housed 14,599 employees in 562 companies and organisations by the end of the period. This park itself is claimed to be worth 6–8 percent of GDP in the Malaga province. It is not clear, though, how many of these firms are genuinely high technology, or have emerged as a consequence of the intervention, as such parks tend to attract existing local firms and often exhibit a high level of deadweight. But, in Nord-Pas-de-Calais, despite investments in new research centres in the 1990s and technology advice to enterprises, the effects on regional R&D levels and patents were limited, and the region's RTD strengths remained primarily public-sector focused. However, since 2007 there has been a new emphasis on innovation with a new platform for innovation focused on growth in private-sector R&D.

What is also striking looking over the entire period is how the approach to innovation evolved between 1989 and 2012. For example, Nordrhein-Westfalen initially focused on technology centres and technology transfer, then moved on to a cluster or competence network development process. Some of the initial technology centres were quite successful, as shown by the growth of micro- and nanotechnology from 925 employees in 1999 to 2,274 in 2008. In North East England, the initial emphasis was on innovation support and advice for SMEs, with a particularly successful collaborative scheme to connect SMEs with experts across the region's five universities. After 2000, the region refocused its innovation support around a small number of key research and commercialisation institutes. The most successful of these were linked to renewable energy and process industries, and are now national centres of excellence, sustained by national funds and private-sector contracts.

Enterprise

Support for enterprise is another theme that became central to regional strategies and programmes over the study period and also became more sophisticated in the forms of intervention. At the core of most regional programmes was a desire to increase the number of SMEs through support for entrepreneurship or to stimulate growth in existing SMEs through support for competitiveness. Although the case studies reported notable achievements in support for SMEs, they also raised doubts about the true additionality of the results, as the following examples indicate.

- In Itä-Suomi, EU programmes committed expenditure aimed at raising productivity, expanding capacity or improving quality, but evaluations have questioned the additionality, as many projects would have gone ahead without support.
- In the 1990s Galicia also provided subsidies for loans to SMEs to support capital investment, with a €194.5 million fund inducing €1.6 billion investment and creating a reported 9,789 jobs, but the main sectors supported included retail as well as food and fishing, again raising questions about deadweight.

Some common approaches appeared to bear fruit. Most regions developed some form of incubators to support new business starts. The effects of business advice have often been difficult to assess as the causal link between the advice offered to the firm and changes made by the firm can be intangible. Some initial business advice schemes worked on the basis of maximising the number of firms assisted, with the level of bespoke advice and support for each firm being limited, and often best characterised as awareness-raising. However, the link from such advice to increased GDP or employment is tenuous, and it is hard to show how much firms made use of such advice. In many cases, the advice simply had no effect; in others, there may have been deadweight as assistance was given to firms that would have grown in any case. More intensive consultancy offered better chances of both stimulating change in the business as well as being able to measure the effects.

Structural Adjustment

All fifteen regions had identified a need for the transformation of their industrial base as a central element of their strategies and hence considerable activity and achievements are concentrated under this thematic heading. This theme also overlaps and complements the innovation and enterprise themes, with evidence of common strategies, as well as support for related infrastructure and labour market initiatives. Structural adjustment strategies can be broadly divided between firm-based and sectoral or cluster-based approaches.

Firm-based approaches ranged from support for specific firms or types of firms, such as restructuring grants, to foreign direct-investment assistance. A striking example of this approach was in Sachsen-Anhalt, which devoted the bulk of its ERDF funding to direct support for restructuring of enterprises such as privatised or newly established private units. Cluster-based approaches tended to encompass a broad range of policies to promote cluster growth including aid to individual firms, dedicated infrastructure and support and advice aimed at the wider cluster. In one form or another, they were adopted by nearly all regions covering a mix of traditional sectors, new technology or knowledge-based sectors and services such as tourism.

Tourism was one of the most popular supported sectors, with all but one of the fifteen regions identifying it as a priority. In most regions, support was focused on visitor attractions (sometimes in the private sector) or marketing, but in a few regions there was direct subsidy for hotel operators. Basilicata focused on the conservation of its natural and cultural heritage and then on the development of the tourism supply chains and marketing activities, as well as investing in improved accommodation. ERDF support for some forms of basic service infrastructure associated with tourism complemented some domestic policy initiatives, such as the restoration of the Sassi di Matera (ancient cave dwellings), although regional actors were critical of inadequate investment in external transport links. The story on tourism is not clear cut though. In some regions and for some niche markets, the ERDF investment helped to develop new tourism and stimulated growth that may not otherwise have taken place. Selected transport investment would certainly have been needed to cope with greater numbers—enlarged airports, new port facilities for cruise ships, for example. Improved internal mobility within regions also helped spread the benefits of tourism into rural areas that had been previously poorly accessible. However, this all took place against the background of rapidly growing tourism industries, driven by general economic growth, low-cost airlines, and easier booking of accommodation via the internet. How much of the growth was purely down to the effects of ERDF is impossible to disentangle, as the effects were cumulative across all of these drivers. It is, however, likely that many of these regions would have found it difficult to accommodate growth without the assistance of the ERDF, and that growth would have been likely to be more concentrated in existing tourism hotspots and probably with a more negative environmental impact.

Regional Infrastructure Endowment

Infrastructure investment also varied in form and scale across the fifteen regions with a strong orientation—and large allocations of resources—towards major transport networks, water and basic and environmental infrastructure (e.g., sewage, water purification) and energy in the Convergence and Phasing-In/Out regions and a greater emphasis on industrial sites and smaller-scale transport projects in the RCE regions. This section deals mainly with transport and broadband infrastructure, whilst water and other environmental infrastructure are discussed under the environmental theme below.

All regions tended to focus on infrastructure in the 1989–1993 period, but there is limited published information on the achievements, although some regions provided some simple output data such as length of roads constructed. The large infrastructure investments in Convergence regions were transformational, developing new highway networks, improving large proportions of existing road networks, building new high-speed rail lines or enhancing metro systems, new water crossings and massive improvements in key airports and ports. They were also central to the intervention logics of successive programmes, leading to fundamental improvements in facilities. The consequence of successive programmes with large infrastructure components has been a cumulative improvement of transport networks beyond that of isolated projects, enabling links across modes—providing improved road and rail links into expanded ports, for example.

Yet there were failings, associated notably with the fact that large additional investments in capital infrastructure create significant increases in operational costs, which may not have been budgeted for, and such costs are excluded from the ERDF. In cases where quality was perhaps sacrificed to complete projects within a programme period, remedial work was subsequently needed. In Andalucía parts of the road network had to be rebuilt, having been built quickly over difficult terrain. A rebuilt section of the A92 motorway was repaired, then reconstructed, and then needed further repair following landslides. Some of the infrastructure built thus was not operating at optimal level, due to the inability to meet operational or maintenance costs—a problem with some waste-water purification plants (again, in Andalucía but also in Campania). These issues were less prevalent in the Objective 2/RCE regions, although some environmental or public realm improvements from the earlier periods have become neglected.

Another problem with infrastructure projects was a tendency at times to spend funding on grandiose or 'political vanity' projects that created excess capacity. An example of this would be an airport built to accommodate many more passengers than would be likely to use it in the foreseeable future. Whilst this could be seen as planning for the long term and anticipating future growth, the additional costs of constructing excess capacity diverted resources within the programmes from other projects or objectives. These issues tended to be more prevalent in Objective 1/Convergence regions with again an example from Andalucía in the form of Malaga airport. Expanded to accommodate 30 million passengers, it handled around 13–14 million per year in 2012–2015. Elsewhere, the European Court of Auditors has found that in nine out of twenty projects audited, one or more projects undertaken were not needed (European Court of Auditors 2014).

The regional benefits of these investments are varied according to the objectives: some were aimed at facilitating greater trade, some at facilitating tourist visitors, some at helping to better connect communities within regions, some at improving quality of life. As illustrations of these chequered results, Campania saw dramatic improvements in public rail networks with the completion of the regional integrated network including the Naples underground, local surface lines and the connection to the high-speed rail network from Rome to Salerno. Journey times to Rome were cut by 38 percent to sixty-five minutes, and local commuting has also become much easier, thereby increasing access to employment. Most of the 139 million passengers per year using the metro network are due to the new facilities built with ERDF support. The consequences for local mobility have been huge—but they are difficult to quantify, despite anecdotal evidence.

The wider investment in new and improved roads, especially within regions, can be better seen in reduced travel times, which have facilitated easier access from rural and suburban locations to employment opportunities in urban areas and better access to hospitals and other public services, and have encouraged tourists to spread out from traditional resorts to more rural areas. There is, however, a question as to whether improved travel times between regions is always beneficial as shorter travel times can mean the peripheral area is more easily served from a core region. Regions had generally not undertaken this form of detailed impact assessment, and improved travel infrastructure was regarded as generally positive. Certainly though, the benefits of new metro/local integrated transport systems in Porto and Naples were clear, simply in terms of the numbers of users, which represents fewer road journeys coupled with increased mobility within the city and shorter commutes. Improved safety was also acknowledged in several regions, with reduced numbers of accidents on railways and roads in Portugal as a result of the replacement of level crossings by bridges. In Naples a reduction of CO_2 emissions was also reported.

Labour Market

Labour market projects have tended to be a minor element within ERDF programmes as these issues were primarily met by European Social Fund (ESF) programmes, or ESF measures within multifund programmes. However, some ERDF measures were targeted at labour market objectives, beyond the general aim to create and support jobs across the mainstream ERDF programmes. Typically, ERDF has been used to support the infrastructure needed to deliver training, such as training centres, and has been measured in terms of the number and floor space of training establishments provided. So, over the 1989–2012 period, projects were developed to provide new multimedia workstations in training facilities, to expand and modernise vocational training centres, and even to support the development of university facilities.

In all of these projects, the evaluation of the results is extremely difficult as the immediate consequences have been the housing of ESF-supported projects, which then have their own results. The main labour market benefits of the ERDF have come from the effects on job creation and preservation in other thematic axes, such as enterprise or infrastructure.

Social Cohesion

The social cohesion theme has also often been the focus of ESF measures, especially in areas where social cohesion is linked with access to labour markets, but the focus here is on social cohesion projects within the ERDF. This involved various types of measures and projects: some were concerned with basic public and social services such as education and health, and others focused more on urban or rural regeneration and community economic development.

The largest social cohesion programmes were concentrated in the Objective 1/Convergence regions where basic public infrastructure provision was supported, such as the building of schools and hospitals. Achievements of this kind took the form of completed or improved facilities leading to a better provision of public services—more patients treated, more students staying in schools for longer. In Andalucía, three new hospitals were built, along with the renovation of many others and also primary health centres. One hundred and three new secondary schools and thirty-four primary schools were built, but also sports facilities such as twenty-three indoor pools and eighteen sports centres, as well as care centres and shelters for the homeless. Such scale of basic public service provision was the case in several of the Convergence regions and has clear social benefits as well as an economic impact. For example, enhancement of health care in Basilicata led to a marked reduction in the number of people having to seek treatment outside the region.

At the softer end of the scale were programmes for community economic development in the Objective 2/RCE regions. Here, the nature of projects was much wider and tended to focus more on building social capital in deprived areas and helping to lay the foundations for people to get back into work, often in the social enterprise sector. Community projects were often quite small, limited in some cases by the ability of the third sector to provide matched funding, and hence achievements were limited. A particular issue in this theme is whether such small projects were effective at generating achievements, although they were often good at leveraging voluntary resources and reaching groups that would not otherwise have been engaged in the Structural Funds.

Environmental Sustainability

Sustainability as a theme varied considerably in scale depending on the degree to which a region needed to build or renovate its waste and water infrastructures. Hence, a major focus of effort and achievements was on the provision of clean water and the installation of waste-water treatment. Another environmental problem, addressed in several regions, was derelict or contaminated land, especially due to old industries such as mining and steel. Other major elements of this theme included the preservation of natural environments and investment in renewable energy, clean technologies and CO_2 reduction.

Investment in water resources was particularly important in the Convergence regions, whereas the major problem in the old industrial regions was derelict and polluted land. Several regions also supported the creation of new national parks and nature reserves, or environmental projects to protect natural areas. The results of such projects were generally not amenable to quantification as they ranged from the protection of biodiversity to the enhancement of public spaces such as beaches and parks. The benefits of environmental improvement tended to be focused on quality of life, particularly in terms of the local environment, with cleaner waterways and restored natural areas, as well as the reduction in possible risks to the human population from pollution and unsafe water supplies. 'Green' jobs were also created: for example in Andalucía it was estimated that in 2000–2006, support for the protection and regeneration of the natural environment helped to generate 34,790 jobs in construction, and to maintain 1,095 jobs.

Spatial Distribution of Economic Activity

Rebalancing development across the territory was prominent in many programmes, albeit with a relatively small share of expenditure. In many of the case-study regions, internal inequalities were a concern, whether between more and less developed areas, between urban and rural areas, or between a core and periphery relating to access, or to a coastline. Although there were almost no specific measures identified as being purely about territorial rebalancing, most regions could identify some form of intraregional territorial impact arising from the programmes as a whole. In some instances, EU programmes exacerbated spatial inequalities as investments were concentrated in more urban areas or areas that had greatest potential to absorb funding. There may have been measures with the objectives of offsetting such effects, but these were often smaller in scale—such as community development actions. Itä-Suomi, for example, experienced continued drift of population and economic activity towards the cities. Similarly, in Burgenland, the relatively weaker south of the region was not able to reverse emigration trends or achieve significant catch-up despite receiving the highest intensity of ERDF support. Its ERDF receipts were 141 percent of the regional average, compared with 83 percent in the north of the region, which facilitated the growth of new economic sectors such as renewable energy and tourism.

OVERALL ASSESSMENT
OF ACHIEVEMENTS AND 'WHAT WORKS'

Although there are difficulties in assessing the aggregate achievements of programmes, it is clear from the available data and the qualitative assessment that there have been considerable areas of success, as well as disappointments. Achievement indicators improved over successive programme periods; by 2012, all programmes were using output indicators and there was a growing use of results indicators, but many problems remained. In part, these problems relate to the setting of appropriate targets against well-developed intervention logics, but were also due to poor definition of indicators, weaknesses in recording outputs and simplistic aggregation. The nature of programmes with diverse interventions also made the setting of consistent indicators difficult, both within and between regions.

While aggregate quantification of achievements is difficult or impossible at the level of the region, let alone across regions, the qualitative assessments of achievements provide some insights. In particular, they provide more detailed understanding of the development paths pursued by individual regions, for example, the shifts in innovation investment from building up public research capacity to include business R&D, innovation support and science parks as part of regional innovation strategies, or from generic business aid to improving the business environment.

The research also provides some indication of 'what works'. Some large infrastructure, environmental and social cohesion investments in Convergence regions have been transformational, in terms of improved accessibility, increased standard of living through better housing, better-quality healthcare, connection to water supply and sewage networks, and environmental remediation (such as of derelict or contaminated land). Such initiatives were central to the intervention logics of successive programmes. By contrast, the fragmentation of interventions (e.g., of innovation support) reduced achievements in economic development compared to the focusing of research/innovation on key themes or centres. The value of a systemic or holistic approach to interventions is evident in some regions, especially in the provision of enterprise support, integrated territorial development schemes, (some) financial instruments and cluster-based strategies such as investment in tourist and cultural facilities to promote change in image and tourist flows.

Conversely, the assessment of achievements highlights problems with strategies, notably:

- insufficient consideration given to the additionality of interventions and deadweight (e.g., in enterprise support);
- a lack of prioritisation of interventions, especially in the failure to concentrate support to achieve critical mass;
- insufficient clarity on the time periods over which certain interventions can be expected to be effective and yield results—the long-term benefits of certain kinds of intervention (e.g., university investment) were elusive in the absence of linkages with other aspects of economic development;
- the balance between public- and private-sector investment at different stages of economic development strategy—particularly an initial emphasis on public investment for innovation that was only later followed by support for innovation in industry;
- the degree of sustainability of interventions, in terms of funding (e.g. underutilisation or over-expensive maintenance costs of physical infrastructure, underestimated operational costs of investment in cultural facilities);
- inadequate consideration of the appropriate scale of investment, especially with regard to community-development projects or renewable-energy initiatives; and
- insufficient attention to the spatial or territorial cohesion of regions—the spatial concentration of investment (often associated with scope for spending funds) has widened disparities or inequality within several regions.

FROM ACHIEVEMENTS TO EFFECTIVENESS

Although much has been achieved as a result of Cohesion policy in the fifteen regions, a crucial evaluation question is whether the outputs and results fulfilled the objectives set when the programme was formulated: this constitutes effectiveness. Objectives may be explicitly set out in programme strategies, possibly with specific targets for outputs, but are often also implicit and therefore have to be imputed. For this study, as noted earlier, *effectiveness* is defined as the extent to which programme objectives were achieved, distinguishing, where relevant, between explicit objectives stated in programme documents and those imputed by the research team. Effectiveness can be assessed both by looking at the achievements in relation to the overarching goals of programmes and, bottom-up, by appraising the targets relating to specific measures and/ or priorities.

The variety of regions, programmes and contexts means it is likely that some will be successful and some will have experienced considerable problems. Effectiveness can be judged at several different levels and in terms of different forms of intervention.

- Programmes have overarching or programme-level objectives, usually set as a small number of overall goals that may be a mix of qualitative and quantitative objectives. These might be as generic as improving the quality of life or much more precise, such as creating a specified number of jobs.
- Within programmes there are usually objectives and targets for specific measures or themes, which again may be a mix of qualitative and quantitative objectives. Here a measure may have a greater range of targets depending on the variety of actions anticipated.
- At the level of individual projects, there are objectives that will be expected to contribute to measure objectives, but may include additional objectives not anticipated in the original programme.

A first exercise makes use of ordinal correlations to explore whether there is a 'pair-wise' correspondence between the objectives and achievements of the programmes in the fifteen regions over the period from 1989 to the present (see table 6.1). This relatively simple statistical technique has been employed to translate the qualitative assessments

Table 6.1. Relationship between achievements and objectives (ordinal correlation)

		1989–1993	1994–1999	2000–2006	2007–2013	All periods
All thematic axes	Number of obs	104	120	120	120	120
	Spearman's rho	**0.672**	**0.421**	**0.405**	**0.193**	**0.518**
	Prob > |t|	0 ***	0 ***	0 ***	0.0348 **	0 ***
Enterprise	Number of obs	13	15	15	15	15
	Spearman's rho	**0.490**	**0.093**	**0.250**	**0.268**	**0.369**
	Prob > |t|	0.0894 *	0.7406	0.3692	0.3348	0.1754
Structural adjustment	Number of obs	13	15	15	15	15
	Spearman's rho	**0.597**	**0.345**	**0.320**	**0.133**	**0.791**
	Prob > |t|	0.0312 **	0.2077	0.2456	0.6374	0.0004 ***
Innovation	Number of obs	13	15	15	15	15
	Spearman's rho	**0.325**	**0.106**	**-0.321**	**-0.104**	**0.392**
	Prob > |t|	0.2784	0.708	0.2431	0.7129	0.1488
Environmental sustainability	Number of obs	13	15	15	15	15
	Spearman's rho	**0.852**	**0.653**	**0.717**	**0.128**	**0.675**
	Prob > |t|	0.0002 ***	0.0083 ***	0.0026 ***	0.6495	0.0058 ***
Labour market	Number of obs	13	15	15	15	15
	Spearman's rho	**0.613**	**0.320**	**0.183**	**0.144**	**0.168**
	Prob > |t|	0.0259 **	0.2456	0.5145	0.6094	0.5489
Social inclusion	Number of obs	13	15	15	15	15
	Spearman's rho	**0.760**	**0.608**	**0.095**	**-0.309**	**0.110**
	Prob > |t|	0.0026 ***	0.0163 **	0.736	0.2626	0.697
Spatial cohesion	Number of obs	13	15	15	15	15
	Spearman's rho	**0.531**	**0.376**	**0.375**	**0.595**	**0.381**
	Prob > |t|	0.0616 *	0.1667	0.1681	0.0192 **	0.1618
Infrastructure	Number of obs	13	15	15	15	15
	Spearman's rho	**0.598**	**0.138**	**0.595**	**0.127**	**0.716**
	Prob > |t|	0.0307 **	0.625	0.0193 **	0.6534	0.0027 ***

Source: Analysis of regional research data collected for the study.

made by the case-study teams into comparative quantitative findings across the fifteen regions. For each region, achievements, objectives and needs were assessed on an ordinal scale for each of the eight thematic axes. Research teams working on the study in each of the regions rated objectives on a five-point scale from those that were a very high priority to those that were not a priority. Similarly, achievements were ranked from very high to very low. It should be noted that because these are the judgements of research teams, based on the mix of research they conducted, there will inevitably be a degree of arbitrariness about the scores assigned. Despite these caveats, the exercise provides a worthwhile overview about effectiveness.

In essence, if there is a positive and statistically significant ordinal correlation, this suggests that the policy intervention can be judged to be effective, whether for the programme overall or in the respective thematic axis of intervention. Thus, if objectives are assessed to be a high priority, and achievements are also assessed as high, there will be a high ordinal correlation that indicates strong effectiveness. By contrast, if one of the pairs is rated as 'high' and the other is rated as 'low', the ordinal correlation will signal ineffectiveness. In particular, if the priority is low, but the achievement is high, this is still to be welcomed, but means that what the programme is achieving is not central to its objectives. Effectiveness, therefore, has to be interpreted as the degree to which high-priority objectives are met, and should not be confused with other possible interpretations such as value for money. In this exercise, all axes are treated as being of equal significance, which means that the aggregate assessment of effectiveness at a programme level is not sensitive to the balance of expenditure across thematic axes.

The findings of this analysis suggest that, overall, the programmes are judged to have been effective. Starting with the whole sample, there is a high, positive and statistically significant correlation between the views on achievements and the imputed objectives for all the axes, assessed for the full twenty-three-year period, from 1989 to 2012. The correlations are also positive and significant for all the axes in the individual programme periods, albeit somewhat lower, though still significant, for the incomplete 2007–2013 period. Several of the case studies reported a degree of convergence or, at least, the arresting of relative decline (North East England and Burgenland). Effectiveness is considered to have been especially high in the 1989–1993 period, in which it is positive and significant for seven out of the eight thematic axes taken individually. In this period, although the monitoring of outputs was poor, many regions prioritised infrastructure and achievements were clearly observable.

Environmental sustainability is the thematic axis with the greatest perceived effectiveness, as shown by the high, positive and significant correlations in the 1989–1993, 1994–1999 and 2000–2006 periods. The correlation is also positive in 1994–1999 for social cohesion, while for regional infrastructural endowment the effectiveness is very high in 2000–2006, and for spatial distribution of economic activity within the region, it peaks in 2007–2013. Nevertheless, some regions, such as Burgenland, were not effective in reducing intraregional disparities. It is also noteworthy that there is no theme or period with a statistically significant negative correlation, meaning that there have been no significant backwash effects in any particular thematic axis or period.

Effectiveness at Programme Level

A second way of looking at programme effectiveness is to examine individual regions. The assessment in the following two sections concentrates on programme-level and measure-level objectives, with emphasis on what makes the difference in the achievement of objectives. The starting point is again the synthesis of the qualitative assessments conducted by the fifteen case-study teams of how effectively programme objectives were achieved.

A particular aim of this assessment is to identify whether there are specific regional issues or types of interventions that detracted from effectiveness. As there are regions with different levels of development, and with different levels of complexity and scale of Structural and Cohesion Funds programmes, systematic differences in effectiveness might be expected. For example, are small, focused programmes more likely to achieve their objectives than large, complex programmes addressing diverse objectives? The thematic analysis of achievements also presents opportunities to examine the effectiveness of different kinds of intervention and to reach some conclusions as to whether the choice of intervention, and decisions about how it is implemented, has consequences for effectiveness.

As anticipated, the case studies present a variety of judgements at programme level, with some being broadly effective whilst others struggled to achieve their objectives. Table 6.2 assesses the level of effectiveness at the regional scale across programmes, indicating whether they achieved their objectives as set at programme level. This is by necessity a crude indicator, but it seeks to differentiate those cases where the programmes as a whole met the objectives set for them. Estimates are not made for the 2007–2013 period as it was too early to judge whether regions would achieve targets at the time of the study, although in most regions the disruptive effects of the period of economic crisis from 2008 until 2012 rendered initial objectives irrelevant.

Table 6.2 shows the shifts over time, with some regions becoming better at meeting targets and others seeing poorer performance. These changes do not necessarily reflect a change in absolute achievements, as the assessment is made against objectives, which themselves change.

Table 6.2.   Programme-level assessment of effectiveness

Region	1989–1993	1994–1999	2000–2006
Algarve	3	3	3
Andalucía	4	4	4
Aquitaine	3	3	3
Basilicata	3	3	3
Burgenland	n/a	3	4
Campania	2	3	2
Dytiki Ellada	2	3	4
Galicia	–	3	4
Ireland	4	4	1
Itä-Suomi	n/a	–	4
Nord-Pas-de-Calais	3	3	3
Nordrhein-Westfalen	–	3	1
Norte	1	1	1
North East England	–	1	4
Sachsen-Anhalt	5	1	5

Source: Project research

Key

5	strongly exceeded objectives	2	underperformed against objectives
4	exceeded objectives	1	strongly underperformed against objectives
3	met objectives	–	insufficient data

This may simply be because one region softened an objective to make it more attainable, while another set more ambitious targets that were less likely to be achieved. This is a general weakness of measures of effectiveness (as defined for this study), as programmes operate within their own world and the setting of objectives and targets can just as equally influence effectiveness as the outputs. Generally, regions became better at setting realistic objectives that were attainable, although this was not the case in a number of regions—notably Norte and Campania—where effectiveness was judged to be poor in all periods.

Quality of life was a particular issue in several regions—often portrayed as a key priority, but rarely specified or quantified, highlighting problems of measurement of very general objectives. In most cases, quality of life was indeed improved, at least for the users of new infrastructures or the beneficiaries of enhanced public services or cultural facilities. Urban and community regeneration also improved the lives of people. However, these reported achievements have not necessarily contributed to the economic changes that were the core objectives.

For most regions and programme periods, the judgement of regional research teams was that programmes more or less achieved their objectives, although with many caveats, as indicated below. In a few cases it seems the programmes exceeded their objectives, such as in Sachsen-Anhalt (which focused on job creation and significantly exceeded its targets in two of the periods) and Ireland (which also exceeded objectives during the 1990s, but missed its targets in the 2000–2006 programme).

Several regions had at least one 'bad' period when objectives were not realised, again often due to overambitious objectives, and a small group of regions had a poor performance overall. In some regions, objectives were set at overambitious levels and as a consequence were not achieved.

Effectiveness at Measure Level

At measure level, the variability of performance increases, with examples of highly successful measures considerably exceeding objectives (at least as measured by targets), and some that largely failed to achieve anything. What is perhaps more important than documenting such variety is to explore the factors behind success and failure at measure level, given that it is the performance of such components that underscores the achievement of programme-level objectives.

There was a generally positive view of the effectiveness of objectives relating to different forms of infrastructure across the regions. Objectives were met, although sometimes only after successive rounds of investment spanning more than one programme period, and infrastructure projects were well delivered and had a good impact on quality of life. Clearly, regions were reasonably assured in their ability to deliver these kinds of projects, although with some reservations.

Business parks also led to mixed results. Although, floor space targets were attainable, the jobs that followed were significantly delayed, often beyond the period of assessment of a programme. Even if there were specific actions to encourage firms to move into new accommodations, this would often be in a different programme to the development of the land and construction of the buildings. Issues of quality affected the results—in Andalucía the rapid construction of roads led to subsequent need for repairs and realignments in later periods. Structural adjustment activities and industrial modernisation were seen as more problematic, and were often slow to yield results, reflecting the difficulties in changing from established industries to new activities. In Campania, support was provided for industrial modernisation, but its objectives were not achieved—possibly due to the labour-replacing effects of capital investment in manufacturing. Support allowed firms to remain in the market (thus safeguarding jobs in the short/medium term), but it did not spur them to become more competitive for the longer term. In several regions, emphasis was placed on safeguarding jobs in industrial sectors when their long-term sustainability may be questionable, even assuming the deadweight effect of such support is ignored.

In Nordrhein-Westfalen, programme authorities were reluctant to make radical changes in approach that might have led to more rapid diversification, and in Nord-Pas-de-Calais the initial emphasis was to preserve existing industrial sectors, only later switching to support for emerging industries. Such considerations had an impact on effectiveness depending on whether safeguarded jobs or new jobs were set as the objective. A focus on new industries might help achieve greater numbers of new jobs, but at the same time trigger a more rapid reduction in jobs in the declining sectors.

Innovation measures also experienced limited short-term effectiveness, but with an expectation of more significant effects in the longer term, suggesting that looking at whether objectives were met within the time span of a single programme (or soon after it ends) may give a misleadingly negative impression. Initial effects, especially where funding was concentrated in the public sector, were often restricted to output measures only. For example, the university sector might grow in line with the level of investment made into university research, but wider growth of RDI in the private sector would be slow to take place, if at all. For example, Basilicata successfully established new research facilities, such as a geodesic research laboratory, supported by domestic as well as ERDF interventions, but there was limited diffusion to the economy as a whole. Better effectiveness was achieved where innovation measures had a greater emphasis on support for the private sector through knowledge-exchange projects and the development of a more sophisticated innovation system. Similarly, regions that had developed a good systemic approach to supporting entrepreneurship, with a mix of policies including incubators, finance, training and encouragement of a wider entrepreneurial culture, reported high effectiveness.

Environmental measures had mixed results, with good effectiveness for land and water reclamation projects, but limited success with clean technologies until most recently. Here, it was clear that most regions had expertise in the restoration of derelict and polluted sites and were able to deliver programmes in that field. But few were able to promote clean technologies effectively in the absence of significant demand or newly established bodies for technology development and knowledge exchange. There is, nevertheless, a positive story to be told about preservation of natural assets in regions such as Basilicata and Aquitaine.

Finally, experience was mixed for social, community and territorial development actions. Conventional interventions such as urban regeneration schemes were generally effective and met objectives, but some of the softer community measures struggled to achieve targets, in part because the sheer diversity of activities did not easily translate into strategic, measurable interventions.

OVERALL ASSESSMENT OF EFFECTIVENESS

The main conclusion from the qualitative assessments of achievements in relation to objectives is that, overall, Cohesion policy intervention over the 1989–2012 period was effective, but with variation by programme period, theme and region. Further, regions are considered to have (mostly) improved their attainment of objectives; in 1989–1993, only six regions were judged to have met or exceeded objectives, for six others it was impossible to make a judgement, and three others underperformed. By contrast, in the 2000–2006 period, most regions met or exceeded their objectives.

With respect to specific areas of intervention, short-term effectiveness appears to be higher for large-scale physical infrastructure, environmental improvements and local business and innovation infrastructure. Regions had difficulty with areas such as structural adjustment, business support, innovation and community development, which required strategies, systems and capacity often found to be lacking. A further difficulty reflected in the overall assessment of effectiveness was the coordination of measures into a coherent strategy.

Most regions had good expertise in capital programmes and were able to set reasonable objectives that were attainable and that were then delivered. However, in those regions with strong infrastructure needs, there were absorption problems in being able to deliver so much so quickly and in being able to guarantee maintenance of the finished schemes. Business support was much more difficult both in setting objectives and in meeting them, and an important success indicator was whether the strategy involved a well-designed systems approach. Regions also had difficulties over structural adjustment in getting the right balance of support for traditional sectors and emphasis on new activities, as well as anticipating the consequences of this balance for targets attached to the objectives. Support for innovation often became focused on public R&D, especially in universities, and successful business innovation depended on the development of an innovation support system oriented to the needs of firms. Lastly, social and community activities were highly problematic in delivery when not tied to infrastructure for core public services such as schools and hospitals.

Chapter Seven

The Relevance of Programmes to Regional Needs

Utility

Whether or not programmes are effective in meeting their objectives, a broader and arguably more fundamental question is whether they succeeded in meeting the needs of the region. For this study, the concept of 'utility' is interpreted as the extent to which programmes led to results that are in line with 'society's needs and the socio-economic problems to be solved', which may differ from the goals explicitly stated in the programmes or that may not have been stated explicitly in the programmes. 'Utility is a very particular evaluation criterion insofar as it makes no reference to the official objectives of the programme' (European Commission 2013a, 35). The concept of utility is particularly valuable where objectives are not explicitly defined or are poorly defined, or when unforeseen effects are anticipated, but is also susceptible to differences of interpretation, precisely because it does not necessarily refer to stated goals.

Possible applications include whether or not Cohesion policy fostered regional development in terms of economic growth, increases in employment and better social and environmental conditions. However, the underlying needs can also be regarded sectorally, so that utility can be judged in terms of improvement in a range of determinants of regional development, such as innovation or accessibility. In either case, the question is whether the needs of the region were met regardless of any strategy or objectives set by the programme.

QUANTITATIVE ASSESSMENT

As with the analysis of effectiveness, a first approach to assessing utility was to analyse ordinal correlations between regional achievements and needs, again based on the qualitative assessments provided by the case-study teams. Ordinal correlations between assessments of needs and achievements provide a broad-brush view of the utility of ERDF policy, and are subject to the same caveats noted in relation to effectiveness in the previous chapter. For utility, the regional research teams were asked to score needs on a scale from 'very high' need to 'very low', recognising that although a need may be present, it may matter much less than others for the development of the region. For example, a dearth of basic infrastructure might be seen as a very high need in a lagging region, whereas social cohesion is not. But as the level of infrastructure improves, there may be an evolution of needs that brings social cohesion to the fore, while further investments in infrastructure are less pressing. The results are shown in table 7.1.

For all periods and all axes taken together, there is a positive and statistically significant correlation between needs and achievement, as assessed by the case-study teams. Although this correlation is not high, it implies that the policy has indeed been useful in meeting regional needs over the long run. Utility is higher for the two first programme periods, while for 2000–2006 the correlation is positive but not statistically significant and for 2007–2013 there is no positive correlation, although it is probably too early to arrive at a firm verdict because at the time of the research it was still incomplete.

Regions tended to think of utility at a thematic level, where specific needs were met (accessibility improved, levels of innovation increased, environmental problems cleared up), rather than aggregate utility, which might be seen in terms of overall convergence with the EU average in GDP, and employment or some other target. Consequently, even unequivocal meeting of needs may not have been sufficient of itself to narrow the gap with the EU average in terms of economic performance as measured by standard macroeconomic variables.

Among the thematic axes, the assessments ascribed high levels of utility to investment in infrastructure. This finding is confirmed in several of the case studies, which note the improvement of accessibility as a key achievement, although incomplete networks mean less utility in

Table 7.1. Relationship between needs and achievements (ordinal correlation)

		1989–1993	1994–1999	2000–2006	2007–2013	All periods
All thematic axes	Number of obs	104	120	120	120	120
	Spearman's rho	**0.345**	**0.195**	**0.120**	**-0.105**	**0.204**
	Prob > |t|	0.0003 ***	0.0332 **	0.1929	0.254	0.0255 **
	Number of obs	13	15	15	15	15
Enterprise	Spearman's rho	**-0.009**	**0.384**	**0.039**	**-0.341**	**0.523**
	Prob > |t|	0.9757	0.1571	0.8901	0.2132	0.0454 **
	Number of obs	13	15	15	15	15
Structural adjustment	Spearman's rho	**0.440**	**-0.061**	**0.112**	**0.138**	**0.141**
	Prob > |t|	0.1323	0.8295	0.6909	0.6231	0.6163
	Number of obs	13	15	15	15	15
Innovation	Spearman's rho	**-0.111**	**-0.147**	**-0.206**	**0.125**	**0.464**
	Prob > |t|	0.7178	0.6014	0.4621	0.6585	0.0811 *
	Number of obs	13	15	15	15	15
Environmental sustainability	Spearman's rho	**0.410**	**0.356**	**0.381**	**-0.018**	**0.172**
	Prob > |t|	0.1637	0.1925	0.1616	0.9482	0.5394
	Number of obs	13	15	15	15	15
Labour market	Spearman's rho	**-0.078**	**0.000**	**0.137**	**0.325**	**0.065**
	Prob > |t|	0.7998	1	0.6273	0.2368	0.8181
	Number of obs	13	15	15	15	15
Social inclusions	Spearman's rho	**0.576**	**0.420**	**0.402**	**-0.218**	**0.166**
	Prob > |t|	0.0392 **	0.1194	0.1377	0.4346	0.5541
	Number of obs	13	15	15	15	15
Spatial Cohesion	Spearman's rho	**0.406**	**0.038**	**-0.161**	**-0.378**	**-0.148**
	Prob > |t|	0.1685	0.8938	0.5672	0.165	0.5979
	Number of obs	13	15	15	15	15
Infrastructure	Spearman's rho	**0.479** *	**0.297**	**0.466** *	**-0.021**	**0.596** **
	Prob > |t|	0.0979	0.2819	0.0798	0.9423	0.019

Source: Analysis of regional research data collected for the study.

some regions. For the enterprise and innovation axes, there is evidence of utility in the long run. Ireland is a good example, where there is a strong legacy in research-based activities.

For the social cohesion thematic axis, utility is high in the first three programme periods but significant only for the 1989–1993 period. There is no theme and no period for which there is a significant negative correlation. Some of the case studies do make clear, however, that much greater emphasis was placed on some themes during different periods. In Aquitaine, for instance, an early focus on jobs and SMEs was considered to be at the expense of other needs, such as for internationalisation of the economy, but later programmes at least partly compensated. In the earlier programmes, the Nord-Pas-de-Calais region was dominated by efforts to cope with the decline of major staple industries.

Selected Indicators of Economic Transformation

The utility of ERDF intervention can, in a manner similar to the analysis of economic performance described in the previous section, also be summarised in charts focusing on indicators that capture different facets of needs. Due to the availability of longer-than-average time series, three indicators were chosen—unemployment, patents (as a measure of the results of R&D) and tourism—each related to at least one of the eight axes of the project (see figures 7.1a, 7.1b, 7.2a, 7.2b, 7.3a and 7.3b, below). They are general indicators and, as such, are influenced by more than one axis. These indicators can be interpreted as results of policy interventions, not being the direct output of any measure or axis.

Unemployment

The unemployment rate is one of the principal direct targets of labour market expenditure, but it is also indirectly influenced by any other expenditure targeting the regional economy, including enterprise and structural adjustment. Unemployment rates in most of the fifteen regions were well above the respective national average (see figures 7.1a and 7.1b), signalling a high need, especially in Sachsen-Anhalt (DEE0 on the chart), Andalucía (ES61) and Campania (ITF3), whose differentials from the national averages were above 12 percent.

Only two regions achieved significant reductions in unemployment gaps relative to their national rates. Sachsen-Anhalt (DEE0) managed

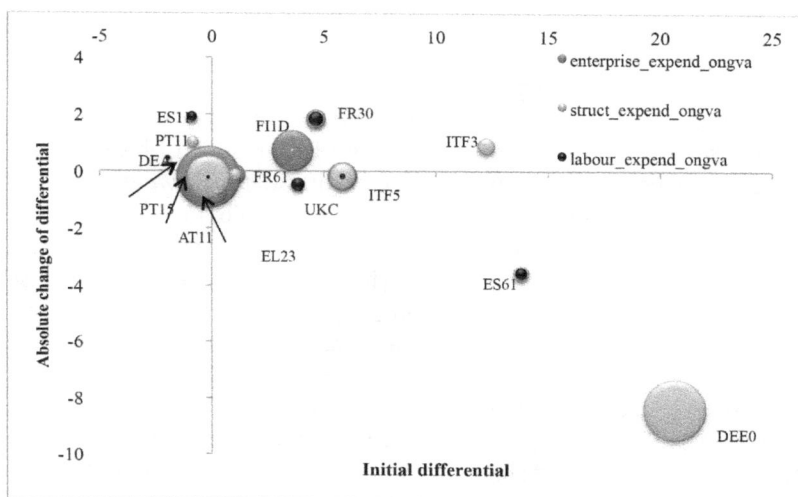

Figure 7.1a.   Relative unemployment rates in programme period 1994–1999
Source: Eurostat and data collected by the research team for this study (analysis by Ugo Fratesi).

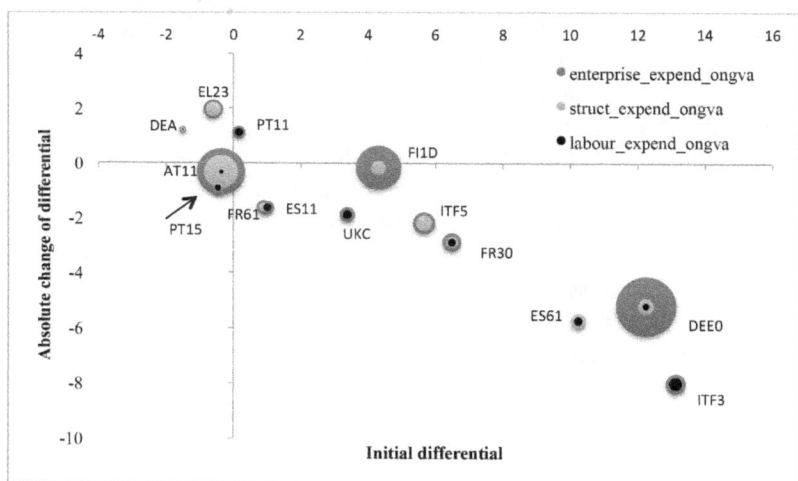

Figure 7.1b.   Relative unemployment rates in programme period 2000–2006
Source: Eurostat and data collected by the research team for this study (analysis by Ugo Fratesi).

to reduce its differential by more than eight points, interestingly despite any investment directly targeting the labour market, albeit with very high investment targeting structural adjustment and, to a lesser extent, enterprise. The other was Andalucía (ES61), which was able to reduce its differential by almost four points, with ERDF support balanced between the labour market and structural adjustment. However this was not sustainable in the economic crisis, and unemployment rose rapidly again. In the other thirteen regions there was little relative improvement, even in Burgenland (AT11) which spent heavily on enterprise and structural adjustment, while some regions went backwards. Nord-Pas-de-Calais (FR30), in which countering unemployment was a core challenge, was unable to make any headway, a result attributable partly to limited success in some of the unemployment black-spots in the region, whereas other centres enjoyed markedly better results. Local concentrations of unemployment were also identified in Nordrhein-Westfalen as a continuing problem, despite ERDF intervention.

The need to curb unemployment was especially prominent at the beginning of the 2000–2006 programme period. Over the subsequent seven years, nine regions were able to achieve a marked reduction in unemployment differentials, while two (Burgenland and Itä-Suomi [FI1D]) improved marginally. Moreover, the regions with the greatest needs achieved the biggest gains, through investments in the labour market but also enterprise and structural change, especially in the cases of Sachsen-Anhalt (DEE0), Basilicata (ITF5) and Nord-Pas-de-Calais. By contrast, two regions that spent heavily on enterprise and structural adjustment (Itä-Suomi and Burgenland), but did not spend significantly on the labour market directly, made no inroads into the gaps. Overall, though, there was more improvement in this period of wider economic growth at a national and international level, although the fragility of this growth is shown by the rising levels of unemployment relative to the EU average for some of these regions since 2008. A sobering judgement on Campania is that the region continued to have the same problems of poverty, unemployment, worklessness, hidden employment and organised crime as it had two decades previously.

Patents

Patents per million inhabitants is a proxy indicator for regional innovativeness (see figures 7.2a and 7.2b), although it is primarily a

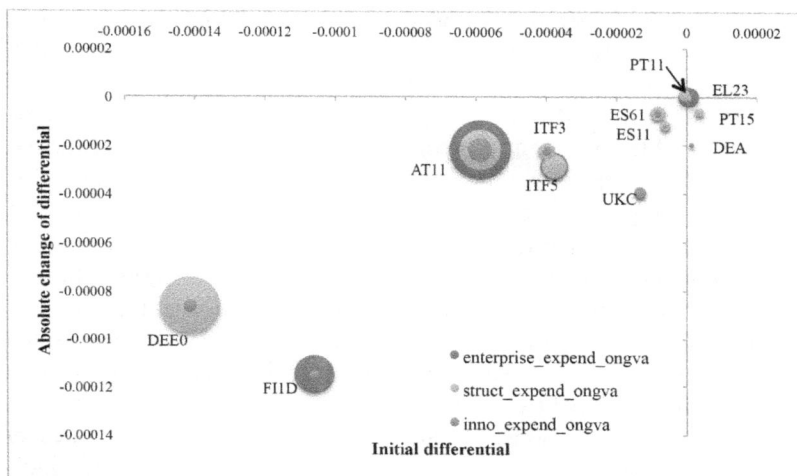

Figure 7.2a.   Relative number of patents per million inhabitants in programme period 1994–1999
Source: Eurostat and data collected by the research team for this study (analysis by Ugo Fratesi).

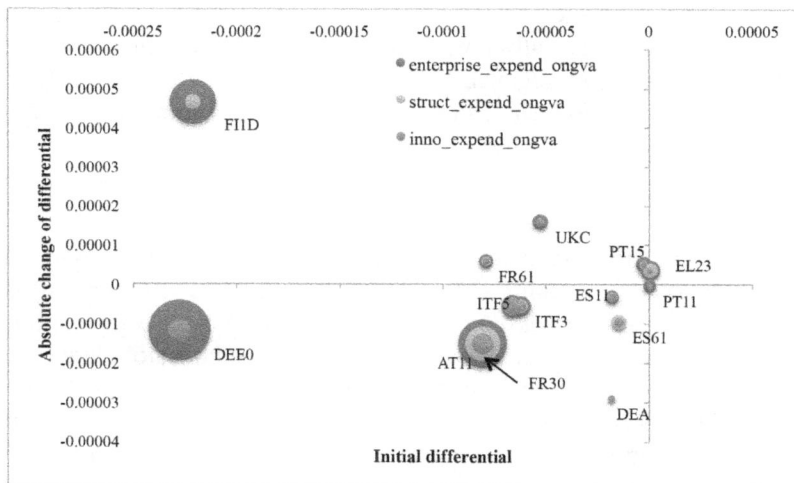

Figure 7.2b.   Relative number of patents per million inhabitants in programme period 2000–2006
Source: Eurostat and data collected by the research team for this study (analysis by Ugo Fratesi).

measurement of inventive activity in high technology sectors, rather than the exploitation of ideas across a wider range of industries. Patents also tend to represent product innovation to a greater extent than process improvements, and many forms of organisational innovation are not eligible for patent protection. Consequently, the indicator has limitations, but there are no other output indicators for innovation with comprehensive spatial and temporal coverage. Some case studies, such as that of Aquitaine, identified major achievements in long-term innovation potential not necessarily captured by the single indicator. Itä-Suomi, similarly, has benefited from a reorientation of the economy towards high-tech sectors, while in Andalucía the ERDF is credited with improving the university sector. Because the analysis is relative to the respective national trends, the findings cannot directly be compared among the fifteen regions. Finland and Germany have high rates of patenting, in contrast to southern member states, so that although individual regions in these two countries may be below the national rates, they may still be high relative to an EU average.

As figures 7.2a and 7.2b show, the needs in terms of innovation were sizeable in 1994 for almost all regions, which were in some cases around the national mean, in other cases lower than the national mean and in other cases much lower. The case-study regions in Austria, Germany and Finland—countries relatively more innovative with respect to the EU—had especially low scores relative to their national means. Moreover, almost all regions, to different extents, performed badly in the 1994–1999 period, since none of them were able to reduce the differential with respect to their country.

Tourism

It is hard to affirm that there is a regional 'need' in relation to tourism, but there are 'opportunities' that could be exploited to improve the regional economic situation, an especially important issue for regions with few other potential growth industries. The indicator here (see figures 7.3a and 7.3b) is the nights spent in tourist accommodation establishments (by residents and non-residents) relative to the resident population, normalised with respect to the national mean to correct for national differences in the scale and cyclical movements of the tourist industry. Expenditure on tourism is included in the structural adjustment axis, but results can also be influenced by expenditure on infrastructure and on environmental sustainability.

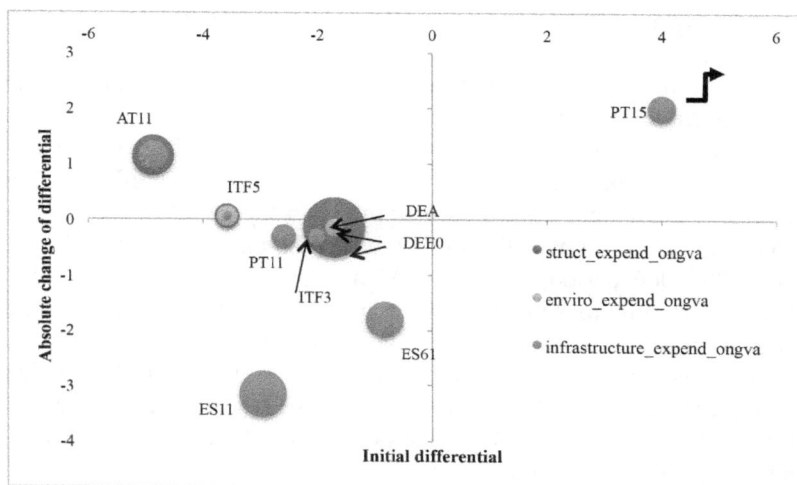

Figure 7.3a. Relative number of nights spent in tourist accommodation establishments (by residents and non-residents) by population in programme period 1994–1999

Source: Eurostat and data collected by the research team for this study (analysis by Ugo Fratesi).

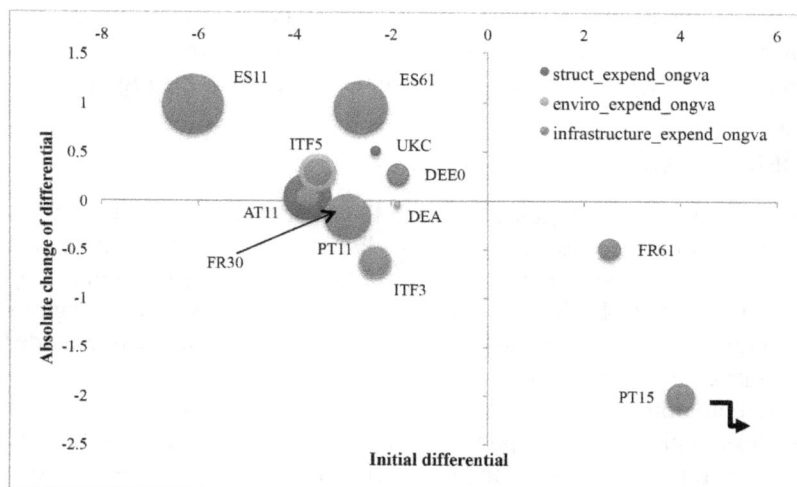

Figure 7.3b. Relative number of nights spent in tourist accommodation establishments (by residents and non-residents) by population in programme period 2000–2006

Source: Eurostat and data collected by the research team for this study (analysis by Ugo Fratesi).

Only Algarve (PT15 on the chart) and Andalucía (ES61), among the fifteen regions, could be regarded as major tourism regions in 1994, indicating unexploited opportunities elsewhere. Burgenland (AT11) made sizeable gains despite being the least tourism-dependent region in Austria at the beginning of the period. It improved its position significantly in a programme period in which it spent significantly on structural adjustment and infrastructure.

On the visitor night indicator, some regions underperformed during the 2000–2006 period, especially Algarve, which lost as much as it gained in the previous period. It is, however, important to note that the strategy in Algarve sought to upgrade the tourist offer towards higher-value tourism, which is not captured by a visitor-night indicator. In this region, the utility is considerable insofar as the research concluded that nearly all the improvements in the last twenty-three years are underpinned by ERDF investment.

QUALITATIVE ASSESSMENT OF UTILITY

As for effectiveness, the utility of policy interventions was investigated qualitatively by soliciting the views of stakeholders and through assessments by the regional research teams; the results are organised according to the categorisation of funding regime in each of the regions.

Objective 1/Convergence Regions

By definition, these regions have had the most extensive needs, and because they have not 'phased out', not all the needs have been met. Some consideration must also be given as to whether the large investments by the ERDF and Cohesion Fund had some negative utility in these regions by putting in place demands on public expenditure that became harder to finance in strained economic times.

A common theme across five of the regions (the exception being Sachsen-Anhalt) is a preponderance of infrastructure investment and support for quality-of-life improvements, and across all these regions these needs were met to some degree. However, the regions also needed to stimulate economic development, transform the industrial base and promote innovation and enterprise. These needs were not always highly prioritised in programme objectives, and investments in infrastructure did not lead to the economic stimuli that were anticipated. Utility has thus been quite low in economic terms across these regions, regarding enterprise, innovation and structural change. Nevertheless, the enhancement of infrastructure tended to bring more benefit to the wider public, through improved public transport networks and roads and personal services (education, health, water quality), as well as some environmental improvements. To this extent, ERDF investment in these regions has a clear utility in meeting some of the needs of the population for improvements in the quality of life, but it has been insufficient to establish self-sustaining growth. As a result, the economic achievements are more fragile and have not provided an adequate foundation for a response to the recent economic downturn.

Tourism was seen as a growth opportunity by all of these regions, but with relatively limited success. In most cases, some of the transport infrastructure had a strong tourism orientation and all invested in tourism attractions and new niche strategies.

Regions Phased Out of Objective 1 Status

Regions that 'phased out' as revealed by a relative gain GDP are all by definition regions that saw significant positive change, whether or not this was the consequence of Cohesion policy.

The region that stands out as having achieved transformational change in 1989–2012 is Ireland (notwithstanding the difficulties encountered since 2008), with its status as a small country having afforded it particular advantages. During the 1990s, the ERDF and Cohesion Fund provided substantial new investment in historically neglected infrastructure such as transport and water, whilst also boosting research and innovation facilities dramatically. This investment helped to support endogenous development but, more importantly, exogenous growth through the attraction of foreign direct investment and can be judged to have responded to the country's needs. The high level of funding during the 1990s coincided with the 'Celtic tiger' period of rapid real growth. Clearly, several other drivers of change were influential, notably the high levels of foreign direct investment, but Cohesion policy facilitated the ability to respond to those opportunities whilst also modernising the indigenous economy (Honohan 1997). Funding dropped after 2000, but ERDF interventions continued to make a positive contribution to development, albeit in a more focused way within a national strategy.

The other regions in this group (Algarve, Basilicata, Burgenland, Itä-Suomi, Nord-Pas-de-Calais) experienced difficulties to varying degrees. An enduring issue are the ramifications of a growing focus on knowledge-based economic strategies for the territorial balance within each of the regions. This was challenging in all these regions, given that they had either significant rural areas or internal disparities. The focus on innovation has reinforced the position of the more urban settlements, exacerbating internal territorial imbalances in Itä-Suomi. This problem, also recognised in some of the other regions, is a conundrum for regions as economic transformation seems to require agglomeration economies that are difficult to replicate in more rural locations. Whilst sectors such as tourism can be developed in the more rural areas, and these six regions have had some success in this, the scope for higher value-added is limited in comparison with the urban areas. Competition in tourism drives down profitability and the typical quality of jobs cannot compare with innovation-intensive sectors that concentrate in the urban cores. Achieving maximum utility at a regional scale may require the acceptance of continued territorial disparities, and the knowledge that policy is one of the causes.

Objective 2/RCE Regions

Some of the regions in this group were those typified by economic restructuring dominated by large, declining traditional industries (e.g., Nordrhein-Westfalen, North East England), while Aquitaine was characterised by an initially small but expanding Objective 2 area coupled with an extensive Objective 5b designation.

The intervention logic for these regions has been one of shifting from an outdated industrial model that had left acute social and environmental legacy problems to embrace new activities and socio-economic structures. These regions mainly faced three broad challenges: to rehabilitate the environment in areas affected by the closure of traditional industries; to convert the economic base to new knowledge-based activities; and to address the social consequences of deindustrialisation. On the first of these challenges, there was considerable success and a high level of utility. Environmental improvement and infrastructure projects, focusing on the reclamation of contaminated and derelict land, had considerable success leading to the restoration of the land either as green space or to be reused for business or residential purposes.

Nordrhein-Westfalen and North East England had severe problems of derelict land, particularly from mining and steelmaking, and these sites had symbolic significance—both negatively as highly visible indicators of industrial decline, but also more positively as icons of regional identity. Both regions were able to gain high utility from the revalorisation of this land, the resolution of ecological problems, the bolstering of cultural heritage, and the change in the regional image to one that was more attractive for new investment and even tourism. The scale of these problems was beyond the resources of local and regional actors and required a coordinated effort involving national government and the Structural Funds. However, the expertise for these types of interventions was well-established, projects were typically well managed and at times innovative, and high utility was achieved.

In meeting the needs of the conversion of the economic base, experiences were more mixed, although improving over the programme periods. In the 2000s, there was evidence of increased utility in economic terms as the regions began to develop more sophisticated systems to support entrepreneurship and innovation, with strong encouragement from the ERDF. New firm formation and growth improved in North East England as the region developed more incubator capacity, reinforced by better links with universities and venture capital, as well as by the promotion of a more entrepreneurial culture. Better targeting of support for growth clusters and sectors also developed in the 2000s, including innovation programmes. Tourism was important, though again with mixed success. However, considering the extreme negative image of earlier years for regions perceived as being dominated by heavy industry, the progress they made in promoting tourism and in developing the creative and cultural industries is indicative of quite strong utility.

Perhaps the weakest area of utility was in dealing with the social challenges. One of the consequences of deindustrialisation has been the concentration of disadvantage in particular communities, with high levels of unemployment, health and social disadvantage, and in some cases poor housing and built environment. In Aquitaine, some rural communities fared less well than the favoured urban centres, highlighting problems of spatial imbalance. Measures to address these issues have been modest in nature, and, as noted above, the effectiveness has often been limited, as indeed has the utility. Here the scale of resources available under the ERDF has been small relative to the scale of the problem, and it is questionable whether it has been worthwhile.

OVERALL ASSESSMENT OF UTILITY

As for effectiveness, the findings on utility are mixed. On the one hand, the ordinal correlations make it clear that achievements are broadly coherent with needs, based on aggregation of the qualitative assessments for the individual regions. Moreover, the fact that this finding is generally corroborated across regions and periods signals that the nature of particular interventions had significant utility. Policy interventions can, to this extent, be judged to be generally appropriate, albeit with the caveat that (as in North East England) while in all periods the region's needs were at least partly met, strategic choices affected the *degree* to which particular needs were met.

The findings on the three selected measures of need are uneven and volatile. Some regions moved from underperforming to exceeding their respective national benchmarks and vice versa, while success in one area (such as tourism) could be offset by a lack of progress on another or an inability to adapt the strategy. In practice, this could be explained by how choices are made on priorities, especially where programmes had relatively limited resources. The Sachsen-Anhalt region, as an illustration, could be criticised as having a one-sided emphasis on fixed assets in the first two programme periods.

The discussion of the three groups of regions according to funding status shows that priorities are, inevitably, also about sequencing, and here there are diverse stories from the fifteen regions. Basilicata appeared to have a better logic of development in the early period, but was pulled towards a less useful approach subsequently. Regions may choose a particular logic of intervention that achieves results in selected areas but fails to deal with needs in others. Such a conclusion should be interpreted as neither surprising nor a strong reason for criticism, because there is only so much that even the best ERDF programme can do. Even so, as the Ireland experience emphasises, the ERDF has left a footprint now widely mainstreamed and often taken for granted, for example, prevalence of multi-annual public-sector investment plans, the use of EU concepts and practices, and widespread acceptance of the role of monitoring and evaluation. This is a dimension of utility that is discussed in the following chapters.

Chapter Eight

Implications for the Design and Implementation of Policies and Programmes

The experiences of the fifteen regions provide extensive evidence on the formulation and implementation of Cohesion policy, with both good and bad practices. Overall, the main message is one of slow improvement in many aspects of ERDF programmes, although problems remain. Indeed, some regions have experienced a deterioration of management or implementation quality in the most recent programmes. Nonetheless, there is increasing adoption of good practice, for instance in the sophistication of strategies (e.g., evidence base, analysis and strategic focus) and programme management (e.g., project selection, monitoring, evaluation). To understand how Cohesion policy functioned, however, it is important to recognise the context for decisions and the prevailing orthodoxies when programmes were launched.

What may be self-evident now about the 1989–1993 programme, for example, was not necessarily obvious at the time. Enhanced sophistication in programming over time has been a requirement of the European Commission, facilitated by learning from previous programmes. What is more interesting is the additional innovation that can emerge from below, but also the barriers that prevent learning taking place in some regions. Against this backdrop, the following chapter summarises the findings and draws out implications of the research for the design of Cohesion policy and the operational programmes through which it is implemented.

THE COHERENCE OF POLICY INTERVENTIONS IN MEETING REGIONAL DEVELOPMENT NEEDS

Although the needs of regions differed and evolved over time, a number of common patterns can be discerned. To recapitulate, in the late 1980s, the main underlying needs can be grouped into four categories:

1. major underdevelopment across all economic, social and environmental indicators;
2. problems related to population sparsity and/or peripherality;
3. a weak economic base, for instance due to transition from a centrally planned economy (Sachsen-Anhalt) or specialisation in agriculture or traditional industries (whether heavy industries or low added value traditional manufacture); and
4. the effects of spatial or labour market disequilibria.

Over time, some regions were able to overcome their initial challenges, others less so. The greatest improvements were realised in the fields of infrastructure for basic public services and transport, and the provision of essential public services. Some needs were not even partially met and indeed, in a few cases, even became worse. For instance, in Sachsen-Anhalt long-term unemployment, weak business start-up rates, poverty and low private R&D deteriorated during the study period, as did poverty in Basilicata and environmental problems in Algarve. Of the various types of need, the most intractable and resistant to policy interventions has been the low levels of private-sector R&D; this was a striking shortcoming in all but two regions in the late 1980s and has since been successfully met only in Ireland among the fifteen regions studied.

This study covers a period of four sets of programmes over twenty years and hence there is an opportunity to examine the way in which programmes have evolved as a result of learning from one to the next. Programme evolution is notable particularly in terms of the ways in which priorities have been identified in relation to an increasingly sophisticated understanding of needs, and changes in those needs.

The concept of strategic regional planning at a regional level was novel to many regions, and in several regions the plans developed for the ERDF were the only or main regional development strategies. These strategies varied within groups of regions, and also within regions between periods, partly linked to their changing ERDF eligibility status.

Overall, there was a general improvement in the analysis of regional problems over the four programme periods with most regions having struggled to bring together suitable data before the 1989–1993 programmes, but making investments in data collection and analysis over subsequent programme cycles. However, the availability of data is only the first step, and regions needed the capacity to make judgements about the real needs and suitable interventions arising from the evidence base. Here, judgements are more contested. Some regions decided that accessibility and communication were the real underlying needs, and these were prioritised accordingly, but such decisions underplayed the importance of changing the productive structure of regions. A decision to address critical transport problems often made sense, but may have had a limited effect on the resilience of the region if the underlying economic base remained unchanged. One possible interpretation is that the opportunity cost of a focus on transport infrastructure may not have been sufficiently taken into consideration in the sense that other, less obvious or immediate investments might have yielded better results.

The Objective 1/Convergence regions along with the southern European Phasing-In/Out regions tended to have wide-ranging strategies, enabled by the financial scale of EU support and the parallel implementation of a range of interventions, comprising not just regional OPs but also sectoral OPs managed by national ministries and domestic programmes. The strategies of these regions focused mainly on the creation of fixed capital, that is, different types of infrastructure, generally supplemented by human capital investment and entrepreneurship and/or industrial development and reconversion support. This emphasis continued throughout the study period, but from 2000 to 2006 with a stronger emphasis on competitiveness and RDI.

The Phasing-In/Out regions in the northern member states had strategies that reflected their diverse development challenges, ranging from peripherality in Itä-Suomi to industrial reconversion in Nord-Pas-de-Calais. Support for business development featured prominently, but there was also some tendency to shift towards social issues and to foster an 'image' change for the region (notably in Nord-Pas-de-Calais). Distinctive strategies were also evident in the Objective 2/RCE regions, partly because lower budgets compared with the much more intensively funded Objective 1/Convergence regions made greater selectivity essential.

Overall trends, insofar as they can be identified for fifteen regions are: a greater emphasis on RDI, particularly from 2000 onwards; the inclusion—over time—of support to integrated urban and community development (initially piloted through the URBAN Community Initiative and subsequently mainstreamed); and a progressive shift in support to tourism. Tourism became a mainstay throughout the programme period of most strategies as a means of economic diversification and structural adjustment, but progressively seen through the lens of the wider attractiveness of regions, underpinned by both cultural and environmental investments.

The study has also attempted to reconstruct the often-implicit development theories underlying programme strategies and in so doing to disentangle the difference between the explicit strategic choices declared in the programme documents and the implicit strategies actually pursued. The difference between the two sets of strategies was particularly evident in the earlier programme periods of the 1990s, when programme strategies were often not linked to sound analyses of needs or evaluation evidence, and they were often generic collections of intervention fields with no clear prioritisation, providing room for differing interpretations and operational choices.

In this respect, two conclusions can be drawn. First, there was little evidence that strategies were underpinned by explicit theories. Especially in the early programmes, strategies were generally drafted as compilations of interventions with no particular overarching rationale. Second, and related, there were often divergences between what was stated in the programmes and what was actually implemented. Generic programmes accommodated diversified local priorities or preferences that were different from what was being promoted by the European Commission or national governments. Often, though, the differences between the strategies stated in the programmes and what was actually implemented derived from the necessity to find pragmatic responses to implementation difficulties, reflected in financial shifts between and within priorities (e.g., in Campania in the 2000–2006 programme in favour of transport infrastructure).

A strategic problem in a number of cases was the lack of integration between national OPs and regional-level programmes, and between national programmes implemented by different ministries. Whilst the idea of national programmes for trans-regional infrastructures makes sense, those countries with a large number of national programmes experienced overlaps and duplication with regional programmes, without effective coordination (examples are the experiences of Basilicata and Campania).

Regional objectives were stable during the 1990s, but underwent substantial changes at the start of the 2000–2006 and 2007–2013 periods, driven mainly by compliance with EU regulatory requirements, and by changes in the eligibility status of regions or parts of regions. The economic crisis of the late 2000s led to extensive reprogramming in a number of regions.

The extent to which objectives were SMART—specific, measurable, attainable, relevant and timely—varied across regions and especially across the period. Insofar as a general trend can be identified, it is that early programmes tended to have generic objectives, that they were not defined and framed in a way that made them measurable, that targets were often absent and expectations overestimated (thus attainability was questionable), and that objectives were not time-bound in the sense of being linked to a realistic operational timetable.

Despite pressure from the European Commission to have credible targets, regions struggled to identify appropriate indicators and were prone to setting targets at levels that were either unrealistic or too modest. As a result, targets were frequently revised down in some of the earlier programmes as it became clear that they were far higher than could be attained. Programme objectives, nevertheless, tended to be relevant, with the main problem being the prioritisation of efforts, rather than the inability of programme authorities to identify needs convincingly.

Nevertheless, the degree to which programme objectives were SMART improved over time, especially the specificity and measurability of objectives, although progress was incremental. The ability of programme authorities to set realistic targets and identify timely paths for implementation remains an area where further improvement is required. A particular problem was the difficulty in estimating a sensible target in advance of knowing the types of project. A target set in the expectation of a particular mix of projects could become unrealistic simply because the projects proposed and selected were of a different character to those anticipated—for example, if offices were built rather than manufacturing or warehouses. But there was also a general difficulty in estimating targets linked to a lack of understanding about what had been the actual achievements of programme interventions in past periods, due to the variable quality of the information provided by programme monitoring systems and the lack of comprehensive, detailed and reliable ex post evaluative evidence.

THEMATIC MIX OF POLICY

The distribution of expenditure across different themes varied by type of region (see figures 5.3, 5.4 and 5.5). As noted earlier, the Objective 1/Convergence regions tended to focus predominantly on basic and transport infrastructure, across all programme periods except for 2007–2013. The proportion ranged from 56 percent of total expenditure in 1989–1993, to 31 percent in 1994–1999 and 2000–2006, falling to a low of 14 percent in 2007–2013. Enterprise support also featured prominently, remaining in the 20–27 percent range from 1994–1999 to 2007–2013, compared to only 5 percent in 1989–1993. The main thematic shift over time was a strengthening of support for social cohesion and the labour market, a trend that started in 2000–2006. The themes of innovation and environmental sustainability remained broadly stable; innovation was allocated 3–4 percent of total expenditure in the 1990s, rising slightly to 7 percent in 2000–2006 and 2007–2013, while environmental sustainability received around 15 percent of total expenditure in the first three programme periods, falling to around 10 percent in 2007–2013.

In the Phasing-In/Out regions, the initial programmes also focused predominantly on infrastructure, which accounted for almost 60 percent of spending in 1989–1993, but became more diversified in subsequent periods. There was a stronger emphasis on enterprise support (34 percent, 38 percent and 21 percent, respectively, in 1994–1999, 2000–2006 and 2007–2013) and, in the 2007–2013 period, structural adjustment and innovation (respectively at 23 and 22 percent of expenditure).

By contrast, in the Objective 2/RCE regions, expenditure was heavily concentrated on enterprise support until 2006 (with this theme accounting for 50 percent of expenditure in 1989–1993, 30 percent in 1994–1999, 35 percent in 2000–2006, but only 15 percent in 2007–

2013) and a marked shift towards innovation and social cohesion in the 2007–2013 period. In this group, two themes received relatively little policy attention throughout the study period: territorial cohesion and the environment. However, whilst the former has progressively diminished (from 10 percent in both 1989–1993 and 1994–1999, to 3 percent in 2000–2006 and no expenditure in 2007–2013), the latter has seen its share double from 2000 to 2006 (from 4 percent to 11 percent of total expenditure).

It was common for the allocation of resources among thematic priorities to shift significantly, but no general pattern could be identified. Instead, the logic reflected both national and regional factors, ranging from political choices to operational difficulties and absorption capacity.

OVERVIEW OF POLICY ACHIEVEMENTS

The broad finding from the qualitative assessments of achievements in relation to programme objectives is that Cohesion policy interventions over the period from 1989 to 2012 were effective, but with variation by programme period, theme and region. Regions are considered to have (mostly) improved their attainment of objectives. In 1989–1993, only six regions were judged to have met or exceeded programme objectives, for six others it was impossible to make a judgement, and three others underperformed. By contrast, in the 2000–2006 period, the majority of regions met or exceeded their objectives. However, these conclusions are subject to important caveats. In particular, the vagueness of programme objectives in some cases involves considerable subjectivity in judging whether they were achieved, and the 'increased effectiveness' of 2000–2006 programmes needs to take account of the frequent reviews of programme targets during implementation (increasing the likely match between expectations and reality).

With respect to specific areas of intervention, effectiveness appears to have been higher for large-scale physical infrastructure, environmental improvements and local business and innovation infrastructure. Regions had difficulty with areas like structural adjustment, business support, innovation and community development, all of which required operational strategies, delivery systems and administrative capacity.

UTILITY OF INTERVENTION

Despite the scale and duration of Cohesion policy support, overall economic performance in most of the regions studied did not improve relative to national or EU trends. It is important to note that this is not necessarily a reason to be critical of Cohesion policy, because turning around an ailing economy is a task that takes decades and, moreover, simply arresting relative decline can be an achievement in itself. To the extent that Cohesion policy has helped supported regions to become 'normal', there is genuine utility.

GDP growth tended to evolve in line with national trends, albeit with a few regions seeing further relative decline (such as Campania and Dytiki Ellada) and only Algarve improving. Some of the regions studied saw noteworthy reductions in unemployment, but Sachsen-Anhalt faced sharp rises of unemployment in the early 1990s, with rates remaining persistently high. In most regions, unemployment tended to follow national cyclical paths, and only one region—Ireland, which is manifestly a special case (see figure 4.1)—experienced a 'virtuous cycle' of higher-than-average growth of both productivity and employment over the period. At the opposite end of the spectrum, only one region, Campania, experienced the 'vicious cycle' of relative decline.

The main conclusion is that, for all periods and for all the themes taken together, the policy has been useful in meeting regional needs over the long run. Interestingly, however, utility is assessed as being higher in the first two programme periods and lower in 2000–2006 (it is too soon to appraise utility for the 2007–2013 programmes), suggesting that the increased sophistication of programmes has not meant improved utility or that it is too soon to make a judgement.

The highest utility was found in the regional infrastructure endowment thematic axis (which mainly comprises transport and telecommunications infrastructure), notwithstanding the lack of resources to fund operational and maintenance costs in some regions, exacerbated by the economic crisis, a consequence that diminishes the utility of investments. A high degree of utility across the study period as a whole was also reported in the fields of enterprise and innovation, whereas only one theme—intraregional territorial cohesion—displays a low long-term utility, with positive assessments only in the first two programme periods.

In most cases, programme resources were not sufficient to address all areas of need. Even so, the fact that in most cases there was only a partial transformation should not be viewed as a criticism: in most if not all case studies, the perception of stakeholders is that the regions would have been worse off had the programmes not occurred, and that the ERDF programmes determined or facilitated a change that saw the regions become better places in which to live, invest or visit. ERDF programmes generally had a transformative effect, but one that has not resulted in growth, productivity and employment, or affected the regions' longer-term resilience. In this sense, the ability of the programmes to stimulate entrepreneurship, induce innovation and support competitiveness appears to have been rather disappointing.

Summarising the utility of Cohesion policy by different types of region, Cohesion policy manifestly facilitated a *transformative effect across the board* in Ireland, delivering considerable improvements in the main areas of regional need and a matching increase in growth and employment. Naturally, the programmes played a role alongside other developments. The positive economic transformation was linked to the integration of the country's economy in wider global markets, across both sides of the Atlantic. This might have an impact on the resilience of the improvements realised, given the country's integration in global economic networks affected by the economic crisis.

In a further group of regions—Algarve, Andalucía and Galicia—the ERDF programmes have delivered a *transformation of the regional economies*, which has indeed been reflected in GDP convergence with the rest of the EU and improved labour market indicators, but which is not proving to have sustainably affected the regions' longer-term development prospects and resilience. In these regions, the ERDF programmes and the Cohesion Fund contributed to major improvements in regional infrastructure endowment and the provision of public services—across all types of infrastructure and services, from transport to schools and hospitals, from water networks and purification plants, to waste collection and recycling, and so on. However, the induced economic transformation was based largely on tourism and services, whereas improvements in productivity and in high-added value clusters were limited to segments of the regional economies that represent relatively small proportions of regional economic activity and employment.

In most of the regions—Aquitaine, Basilicata, Campania, Dytiki El-lada, Norte and Sachsen-Anhalt—the ERDF programmes (and Cohesion Fund in the Greek case) facilitated a *transformation in specific fields*, without having a pronounced wider impact on growth and employment (except in Basilicata) and leaving major needs still unaddressed. In Aquitaine, for instance, improvements were made in developing the image of the regional capital, Bordeaux, and in providing services to the rural areas, with the effect of countering depopulation trends. But, although the programmes have contributed to avoiding a worsening of territorial disparities, they have not been successful at modernising and diversifying the region's productive base, which largely remains reliant on the production of wine, food and trade activities inherited from the past.

Similarly, in Sachsen-Anhalt, there were successes in the fields of structural adjustment and enterprise development, but significant problems—such as a productivity gap, high unemployment levels, low entrepreneurial propensity, poor levels of RDI and a relative low performance of cities in terms of productivity—have still to be addressed. In a similar vein, Basilicata saw major improvements in the provision of basic public services, which were pivotal to develop certain sectors, but without solving the fundamental isolation of the region and altering the overall economic model based largely on agriculture and (increasingly, thanks to the programmes) tourism. Arguably, in regions such as Dytiki Ellada, Campania and Norte, the fact that the transformation achieved was substantial, but limited to specific fields (basic and transport infrastructure and services, quality of life, environmental sustainability), derives from the sheer scale and diversity of the needs to be addressed, and the overall limited scale of the resources mobilised.

In the remaining regions—Burgenland, Nordrhein-Westfalen, North East England, Itä-Suomi and Nord-Pas-de-Calais—the ERDF programmes have had a *positive influence* on wider development factors, supporting change in specific fields, but were unable (understandably, given their moderate scale of intervention) to make a decisive difference to the problems of the regions, and they did not induce a wider transformation of their economies (except to a degree in Burgenland). For instance, in Nordrhein-Westfalen, important achievements were realised in the fields of enterprise and structural adjustment, but unemployment remained high. In Itä-Suomi, the ERDF supported existing domestic policies in the fields of enterprise and innovation, but without facilitating an economic configuration of the region, which remains fundamentally hampered by its isolation within Finland. In Nord-Pas-de-Calais, the programmes enabled a modernisation of certain traditional economic sectors (e.g., transport), promoted new specialisations (ICT) and attracted new investors to the region, but with effects concentrated in the main urban areas of Lille and Arras, thus reinforcing existing intra-regional territorial disparities. In North East England, the programmes successfully promoted a new approach to economic development based on culture and tourism, and improved quality of life through community regeneration projects, but without being able to affect the fundamental shortcomings of the regional economy: low productivity, low entrepreneurship and innovation, high unemployment and worklessness.

Lastly, in Burgenland, the ERDF contributed to advances in GDP per capita and economic performance (although needs persist in most fields except tourism, especially in the south of the region). Burgenland also benefited from the economic performance of Austria, the positive impact of development trends such as the suburbanisation of Vienna, and the effect of domestic interventions in public transport networks.

GOOD AND BAD PRACTICE IN REGIONAL DEVELOPMENT

What constitutes an important contribution to regional development is generally highly context-specific. A key dilemma in most regions was to choose between large, strategic projects and distributing funds across a larger number of smaller, perhaps community-focused projects. It should be noted that the limited size of projects is not per se an element of bad practice and vice versa that large projects are not necessarily the best solution. Interventions in the cultural sphere or grassroots social cohesion projects tend intrinsically to be smaller in scale. What matters is that a degree of critical mass is ensured, in order to achieve the objectives set in programme documents, and this might be better achieved by aggregation rather than larger project size (e.g., the Phlegrean Fields integrated territorial programme in Campania, which was successfully implemented through the integration and coordination of over one hundred projects).

Nevertheless, a problem in some regions was the proliferation of small projects that were not linked cohesively in an overarching framework of how, together, they would contribute to programme objectives. At times, the coordination required exceeded the administrative capacities of regions, resulting in delays or high project mortality, prompting the view that a focused approach was more likely to be effective. Yet in most regions, there was a movement over time towards more strategic use of the funds and in favour of larger projects, partly encouraged by the European Commission threatening to withdraw funding, although problems were also experienced with large projects. Several of the case studies highlighted controversial projects where the value-for-money was disputed, project goals were somewhat unrealistic, or there were significant problems with completing projects to time and budget.

The evidence suggests that ERDF programmes, even when they represent a significant portion of public expenditure in a region (as has been the case historically for most regions characterised by 'major underdevelopment'), achieve more when they complement other investment programmes in the region. For most of the regions, complementarities and synergies were often limited to specific fields or projects, rather than systematically pursued (with the notable exception of Ireland). Even connections between two of the main instruments of Cohesion policy—the ERDF and the Cohesion Fund—were typically found wanting, again with the exception of Ireland, where good cross-fund coordination was ensured by framing Cohesion policy within wider national development policy. Interestingly, the existence of overarching strategies, such as the CSF and NSRF, is not per se a sufficient tool to ensure strategic and operational coherence between funds (and indeed, as the case-study research has uncovered, between national- and regional-level programmes).

Synergies with domestic policies tended to be less problematic, a finding explained by two closely interlinked factors. First, among the largest regional recipients of EU funding, there was strong alignment or integration of ERDF programmes with domestic capital spending programmes. For instance, in Greece around 70 percent of the national Public Investments Programme for the whole 1989–2013 period was allocated to co-finance the national contribution to the Structural Funds. Second, for all programmes the requirement to provide match-funding meant that the ERDF was used to support investments undertaken as part of domestic policies. However, the research revealed that the core Cohesion policy principle of additionality—the expectation that EU funding should add to rather than replace domestic programmes—was increasingly likely to be flouted because of pressures on domestic public spending. An implication is that where Cohesion policy becomes the main source of public investment and has been so for decades, it becomes much harder to separate it from domestic investment.

Chapter Nine

Conclusions

Although its treaty base has been broadly stable since the Single European Act of 1986, which led to the launch of the first programme period in 1989, Cohesion policy is always evolving. With the OPs for the 2014–2020 period now being implemented, attention is already turning to what happens after 2020. Even before completion of the 2016 mid-term review, and its eligibility and budgetary implications, there is already wide-ranging debate on the approach, management and governance of future policy. Central to this is a search for an underlying narrative on the direction of Cohesion policy, along with certain standard dilemmas, such as whether or not the policy should apply to all member states or just the least prosperous countries or regions.

In the aftermath of the severe crises that have afflicted the EU since 2008, the economic context of the next decade will inevitably exert a significant influence. High unemployment and economic stagnation are the immediate manifestations of this legacy, but there is also a need for fresh thinking on how EU policies can contribute to resolving deeper structural problems. For example, the euro crisis saw an upsurge in the emigration of well-qualified workers from several of the southern European countries. Disparities in indicators of innovation also highlight an emerging challenge of coping with a likely divergence in growth dynamics. The persistence of low growth and lack of convergence of lagging regions on the southern and eastern peripheries of the EU poses fundamental questions about European integration.

In parallel, the EU of the 2020s will have to confront other major drivers of change. It will be faced with an intensification of the ageing of the population that will result in a steady decline in the indigenous working population of several member states, aggravated in some cases by substantial net emigration of working-age people. As a result, there will be a need for welfare state provisions to adapt. Coherent policies on both immigration from outside the EU and on mitigating destabilising internal movements are also critical for the political, economic and social stability of the EU—and perhaps even the survival of the Union in its current form. Mitigating climate change and energy security concerns will require substantial investment in networks and alternative capacities.

In all these domains, the EU needs to address awkward governance challenges. Cohesion policy has, latterly, been branded as the investment instrument of the EU, usually associated with the Europe 2020 strategy, yet the latter has lost visibility and may have passed its sell-by date. Indeed, there is an ongoing debate as to whether 'grand strategies' such as the Lisbon Strategy or Europe 2020 are worth the effort, given the limited levers available for ensuring their implementation—apart from being overtaken by economic or political change almost as soon as they are launched.

The launch of the €315 billion European Fund for Strategic Investments (EFSI) with its emphasis on private investment at the riskier end of the spectrum, alongside support for infrastructure networks, points to a different philosophy for boosting growth and jobs. EFSI also has a new governance dimension, demonstrating a desire by the European Commission to be seen to be initiating new policy responses in response to emerging challenges. Following on from the decision to divert money from the Cohesion policy budget to fund the Connecting Europe initiative, as well as the Youth Employment Initiative, the European Commission (supported by the European Parliament) plainly has a taste for taking the lead on new policies and is likely to seek further opportunities to have control of budgetary resources for its own priorities, most likely at the expense of the traditional territorial dimension of Cohesion policy.

The European Structural and Investment Funds (ESIF, a confusingly similar acronym) will, plainly, retain a crucial role in supporting public investment, especially in lagging regions. However, the coherence of their relationship with the wider EU investment strategy, as well as with the more immediate governance procedures of the European Semester and the range of developments envisaged to complete economic and monetary union (European Commission 2015a, 2015b), will not be easy to assure.

This chapter discusses some of the big policy choices that the EU will have to face in the pursuit of cohesion after 2020. It starts by reviewing some of the main questions that will have to be addressed in formulating policy objectives and the tensions behind them. It then examines the place of Cohesion policy in economic governance and looks at whether the smart specialisation paradigm can be the basis for a new narrative. The penultimate section of the chapter assesses implementation difficulties and considers some of the ways of alleviating them. Key messages from the volume complete these conclusions.

KEY QUESTIONS

Several questions were posed by European Commissioner Corina Crețu (2015) about the future of Cohesion policy, adding to those already raised in the sixth Cohesion Report (European Commission 2014). Insights from the experience of the fifteen regions examined in this volume can provide a basis for answering some of them. Her questions are set out in textbox 9.1, and potential answers to some of them are provided in this section under five main headings.

Ultimately, a policy is neither about territories, which are an artificial construct, nor about macroeconomic indicators such as GDP per head, but about the ordinary citizens in those territories and whether they benefit, and perceive that they benefit, from it. Some of the improvements supported by Cohesion policy in basic services, such as water quality, described in earlier chapters have an undeniable impact on quality of life. Yet, even if a sizeable proportion of the funding for such projects comes from the various Cohesion policy funds, the benefits may not be visible on the ground and are often conflated with domestic policy interventions. The risk in this regard is that, if European added value is not evident, it may undermine the political case for persevering with a policy across all member states.

To some extent, the crisis years have seen Cohesion policy used to substitute for heavily constrained domestic budgets in maintaining

BOX 9.1.
COMMISSIONER CREȚU QUESTIONS TO GUIDE
THE POST-2020 COHESION POLICY REFLECTIONS

Objectives
1. How can EU Cohesion best contribute to its two complementary objectives, the two sides of its coin: competitiveness and cohesion? In your opinion, what is the added value of Cohesion policy in this context?

Less-developed regions
2. What is the best way to support the lagging regions, especially those that, in spite of decades of EU and national support, did not converge towards the EU average?

Policy architecture
3. How should the architecture of the policy be defined? Should Cohesion policy continue to invest in the advanced regions, especially in the metropolitan ones, which are not only richer but also privileged by private investors?

Financial instruments
4. What is the best use of Cohesion policy funds to stimulate investment in Europe? Which form of support is most efficient: grants, repayable assistance, financial instruments, or their combination? Should the share of financial instruments in EU funds be further increased?

Thematic and territorial balance
5. How can Cohesion policy investment best contribute to overarching European priorities, while keeping its territorial focus? Should we pay more specific attention to certain geographical areas?

Challenges
6. How could Cohesion policy address new or growing challenges (such as, for instance, energy security or migration)?

Urban dimension
7. What should be the role of the urban dimension in Cohesion policy? Where can EU action bring the most added value? On the contrary, how can Cohesion policy better support growth, jobs and innovation outside heavily populated areas?

Governance
8. How can we further simplify the implementation of the policy for beneficiaries? How can Cohesion policy stimulate better national and regional governance? Should the shared management model be revised? Should there be any kind of conditionality regarding quality of institutions?

Financial allocations
9. Should the allocation of Cohesion policy funds continue to be based on GDP per head, or rather on other indicators capturing social progress?

Economic governance and structural reform
10. What form should the contribution/integration of Cohesion policy to the EU's economic governance and structural reform agenda take?

Source: C. Crețu (2015) speech at the 55th Congress of the European Regional Science Association in Lisbon, Portugal, 28 August 2015.

public investment, even though this is technically at odds with the principle of additionality. Although the crisis has eased, the constraints on public spending are likely to endure, such that just maintaining adequate public investment may have to become a more prominent facet of Cohesion policy, echoing the original rationale for introducing the Cohesion Fund in 1993.

THE OBJECTIVES AND FOCUS OF THE POLICY

A focus on territorial development will always be crucial for the simple reason that it is what the treaty article requires. However, the integration of overarching goals associated with the Lisbon and Europe 2020 strategies since 2007 broadens the policy mandate in ways that unavoidably affect the elaboration and implementation of programmes. In addition, the identification of 'good governance' as a vital element for delivery of more effective policy has ramifications for institutional development. The evidence presented in earlier chapters shows that institutional shortcomings can have damaging consequences for implementation and, thus, that enhancing the quality of public administration is crucial as an underlying objective.

Two dimensions emerge from the evidence as especially important. The first is that regions need a coherent and well-founded long-term strategy, centred on the sources of growth and development, but also capable of adapting to evolving conditions. Second, appropriate sequencing is needed to enable programmes to shift their emphasis as different 'milestones' are reached. The multi-level and multi-annual approach to governance inherent in the Cohesion policy model is widely considered to be an advantage, but a message from this study is that it cannot be taken for granted and needs constant attention. If the national and regional levels operate independently or are at loggerheads, the scope for synergy and coherence will be much diminished. Equally, there has to be better communication and engagement from the EU level on how EU-wide goals translate into the priorities that regions select. In part, this is about 'ownership' of the policy and reconciliation of divergent views on the contributions of individual projects to the aggregate development effort. It also requires a rethink of the process of formulating EU-level objectives and the need for there to be bottom-up inputs from countries and regions.

A new concern—that was already manifesting itself in the 2007–2013 programmes examined in this study—is how Cohesion policy will be shaped by the crisis. The close association with the Europe 2020 strategy in the 2014–2020 period could be challenged for two distinct reasons. First, the strategy itself has lost visibility in the last two or three years as policymakers have concentrated on crisis management and on shorter-term goals. Indeed, Cohesion policy has, albeit to a limited extent, acquired an additional role in macroeconomic stabilisation. By bringing forward spending or relaxing co-financing requirements, this has helped to avoid even more drastic cuts in public investment in member states facing the most demanding adjustment challenges.

The potentially more disturbing second concern is that the gains in economic development ascribed to Cohesion policy over the long-term may be brittle. The evidence is still tentative, but regional divergence is again increasing and the findings for some of the fifteen regions point to a lack of resilience in what has become a more austere economic climate. Although the diversity of experience revealed in earlier chapters invites caution about generalisation, Commissioner Crețu and DG Regio are concerned about two classes of regions: the lowest-income regions in Bulgaria, Hungary, Poland and Romania; and the regions of southern Europe that failed to converge towards the EU average in the 2000–2013 period. While only the latter are represented in this study, the implications for future policy are likely to be similar. Options include greater geographical concentration of funding in these regions and a greater emphasis on growth and jobs (possibly at the expense of other thematic priorities), but might also encompass stricter conditionality about the reforms to public administration and investment in administrative capacity-building that need to be in place, how funding is used, and closer oversight of programme implementation. The latter option would undoubtedly cause friction by curbing the autonomy of the regional level.

There is also an open question about whether, and if so how, Cohesion policy should try to deal with problems currently high on the agenda such as migration and energy security. A dilemma in this regard is that a Cohesion policy that targets the broader EU objectives risks being spread too thinly, yet such breadth can deter threats of cuts in cohesion spending by broadening its reach and political appeal. Earmarking of financial envelopes for specific purposes has been a feature in recent years as Cohesion policy has sought mechanisms to reconcile proliferating demands, but has the obvious drawback of engendering expectations that a policy that needs a consistent strategic framework can be redirected at short notice. There is also a risk that programmes will be interrupted for reasons unrelated to cohesion objectives, such as coping with the high level of migrants entering the union. Both the Austrian chancellor, Werner Faymann, and Germany's interior minister, Thomas de Mazière, have called for less EU funding for countries refusing mandatory migrant quotas (Mendez and Bachtler 2015).

POLICY TENSIONS

The multiple goals of Cohesion policy are difficult to reconcile and will be expected again to feature prominently in the debates on the added value of the policy and how the policy should change after 2020. One such tension is between the traditional objectives associated with territorial development and the strategic aims, which as the discussion in chapter 5 shows, became increasingly prominent in recent programmes. Even within the territorial objectives, Cohesion policy has often struggled to strike a balance between different sorts of needs. Urban, remote, rural, mountainous and sparely populated regions are only some of the spatial categories that have been mentioned in the past.

The ambiguity resulting from unresolved tensions can allow policy actors (at all levels) to exploit the uncertainties to pursue their own, sometimes idiosyncratic, interests, often with little regard to underlying goals of catching up, or better value for money for the taxpayer. What can become lost in this process is coherence in the logic of intervention. Cohesion policy has to be founded on a credible 'theory' of development: what is the rationale for intervention and how will it benefit the territory in which it is undertaken? A lesson from the case studies is that confusion about the logic tends to detract from both the effectiveness and utility of what are often substantial public investments.

EU ECONOMIC GOVERNANCE AND COHESION POLICY

Although successive rounds of EU budget negotiations have seen attempts by some governments to reduce the amounts provided for Cohesion policy, they have largely been resisted. However, for the period beyond 2020, there can be no doubt that the issue will again arise. In addition to the extensive reforms of economic governance of recent years and the legacy left by the crises, especially in some of the lower-income countries of southern Europe, the effects of the growing migration into the EU are also likely to affect future policy choices.

Connections between wider post-crisis reform of economic governance and the conduct of Cohesion policy become contentious when the issue of conditionality arises. There were hard-fought battles around the 2014–2020 regulations governing Cohesion policy, with both the European Parliament and the Committee of the Regions opposing tough macroeconomic conditionality. Nevertheless, the next stages of governance reform laid out in the Five Presidents' Report (Juncker et al. 2015) and in a subsequent communication published by the commission (European Commission 2015b) will see these debates continue. However, fresh thought is needed about the incentives associated with conditionality, how they apply to actors at different levels and their effectiveness.

One of the main objections to macroeconomic conditionality, with the implicit threat of withholding cohesion funding from member states that breach rules on fiscal discipline, is that regions would be penalised for something over which they had no control. A much more constructive approach, already canvassed by a conditionality task force in the run-up to the 2013 reform (Mendez and Bachtler 2015) would be to consider rewarding compliant policies, for example by easing co-funding requirements or allocating funds from a performance reserve disproportionately to good performers. The latter approach was tried in Italy during the 2000s and Basilicata was a region that not only benefited from it financially, but clearly also had the incentive to pursue better policies. The difficulty is that most member states resist what can appear to be interference in their structural policies. Even so, it is worth noting a recent provision for relaxation of obligations under the Stability and Growth Pact for governments that agree to make funding available for the EFSI.

INNOVATION AND CONDITIONALITY

At the heart of the last three reforms of Cohesion policy is the need for stronger support for innovation. There have been concerns since the mid-1990s that support for innovation through the use of ERDF might not always be well targeted on the development needs of regional economies. In the mid-1990s, the Regional Innovation Strategy programme was introduced by DG Regio to help regions identify their innovation needs and develop suitable strategies within their regional programmes, and various forms of advice have been available on and off throughout the period since (Landabaso and Reid 1999). However, despite such support and guidance, there has been a continuing concern that regions and member states have used ERDF to support general research investments that have had limited benefits in terms of productive activities. The research reported in this volume found this was particularly the case in some of the southern European countries, but that even in RCE (more-developed) regions the effects of innovation support have often been short-lived and unfocused.

DG Regio has recognised the importance of innovation to the transformation of regional economies, particularly since the Lisbon agenda, and most recently has adopted the smart specialisation concept developed by Dominique Foray and the Knowledge for Growth expert group. Although the idea of smart specialisation was initially developed out of the need to understand why Europe as a whole was lagging behind the United States in innovation and competitiveness, it was later adapted to fit the development of regional innovation strategy (Foray et al. 2011).

The interest in smart specialisation as a driver of regional innovation coincided with the introduction of the principle of conditionality, and the presence of a Regional Innovation Smart Specialisation Strategy (RIS3) was made a condition of using ERDF to support innovation. The European Commission has supported this through the development of a Smart Specialisation Platform based at the Joint Research Centre—Institute for Prospective and Technological Studies—which has provided guidance for regions on a website and through a series of workshops and peer review processes. Regions were required to submit their smart specialisation strategies (S3s) for review, and a process of negotiation preceded their final approval (Charles et al. 2012).

As regions and countries are now implementing smart specialisation strategies within the 2014–2020 programmes, a number of problems are emerging from this approach—some of which echo the problems of previous rounds of innovation support discussed in this volume. First, there is confusion over what smart specialisation strategies require. As the concept is new and has not been tested in practice, the definition of the concept continues to shift, with some regions seeking to define their existing policies as smart specialisation. Foray has recently suggested that smart specialisation should be implemented through relatively small-scale and short-term projects in which groups of firms and other institutions seek to implement innovations that might lead to new industry opportunities (Foray et al. 2011). This is quite different from previous cluster approaches and an emphasis on building enduring innovation infrastructures.

Second, by making an S3 a condition of funding, even though the concept had not been fully defined, the Commission has essentially forced regions to present strategies that pay lip service to the framework even though the region may not fully understand what is required. It may be that a speculative smart specialisation strategy is a less effective approach than a better understood but more traditional regional innovation strategy. In the absence of experience of what works in practice, it is not clear whether the condition really encourages good programme design and effective projects. The evidence will only emerge over the life of the programme, and hence this is a very expensive experiment.

Third, there is the danger that the baby is thrown out with the bathwater and effective projects from the previous programmes are discontinued because they are not perceived as fitting with smart specialisation. The evidence from this and many previous studies is that regional innovation systems take many years, even decades, to emerge, and the focus on smart specialisation on shorter-term projects rather than building institutions may undermine existing efforts.

IMPLEMENTATION DIFFICULTIES

What ultimately matters to those in a region benefiting from Cohesion policy is whether it delivers, in the two senses of effectiveness and utility used throughout this volume. The evidence presented shows not only that there are big differences in these achievements, but also that shortcomings in implementation are often crucial. Certain themes recur with almost worrying regularity, among which simplification is the most intractable.

There is almost universal agreement that the administration of Cohesion policy should be simplified, and it has been the subject of repeated attempts to oblige, including for the 2014–2020 period. Yet the perception of many national and regional authorities—and often the reality— is that the tendency is still for matters to become worse. According to Mendez and Bachtler (2015, 33) the problem is

> that the regulations and accompanying acts have become more complex and that the administrative workload and cost in managing the funds is greater. The Commission have previously acknowledged that the priority of the reform was to simplify administration for the beneficiaries (especially through measures on simplified costs, document retention or e-cohesion), rather than for Managing Authorities and Intermediate Bodies—which in the view of many member states are facing more complex administrative tasks.

What this finding reveals is that there is often a conflict between simplification aims and that this makes it difficult to please all stakeholders while continuing to satisfy auditing and monitoring obligations demanded by the EU's paymasters. *Transparency* and *accountability* are words that resonate with decision-makers and citizens alike, but in Cohesion policy they are prone to be bandied around rather carelessly. It can be difficult to establish how programmes are devised and who is accountable for which choices. Some of the reforms introduced for the 2014–2020 period highlight the dilemmas between the application of the eminently sound principles of effective financial management, a result orientation and simplification, and the reality in which they are put into practice. A striking example concerns the partnership principle, most recently with a Partnership Code of Conduct. The rules have become more and more ambitious, yet pay little attention to the real hurdles of delivering them on the ground—asking for more even when the evidence suggests that existing requirements were poorly met.

The shared management model is considered to be valid, in principle, for the conduct of Cohesion policy, but to be bedevilled in practice by rigidities and a propensity towards a one-size-fits-all approach. To alleviate these drawbacks, options include placing more trust in member state systems, especially where they have established a solid track record, and putting more emphasis on preventing errors rather than punishing them. In parallel, the Commission could shift the balance of its actions more towards supporting policy implementation, and away from what has been, perhaps excessively, a control function. The scope for introducing a differentiated approach to Structural Funds management is likely to be one of the key issues in debates on the policy beyond 2020.

A complementary answer to improved administration would be to reinforce efforts to boost institutional capacity, reflecting the finding of the present study and the strong message in the Sixth Cohesion Report about its importance for effective policy implementation (European Commission 2014). One imaginative way forward, requiring political will more than explicit funding, could be to stimulate further initiatives to facilitate exchange of good practice among management authorities. These could be modelled on the DG Regio peer-to-peer[1] scheme, but there may also be scope for drawing on the experience of the EU's employment strategies in which more extensive use has been made of constructive peer reviews and exchange of experience.

FINANCIAL ALLOCATIONS,
MECHANISMS AND ELIGIBILITY RULES

Partly as a result of the shift towards achieving EU-wide aims and the consequent need to allocate funding everywhere, the proportion of Cohesion policy funding allocated to regions with a GDP per head below the 75 percent benchmark is at its lowest since the major reforms of 1989. In the 1989–1993 period, nearly three-quarters of the resources went to the Objective 1 regions, but in the current period the proportion is down to just over 50 percent. Although regional designations have become more nuanced, notably with the emergence of Transition regions, the implications of giving less prominence to the least-favoured regions deserve attention. Two alternative models are to revert to a concentration on the poorest regions, wherever they may be, or instead to use relative national prosperity as the key for distributing funds. In the EU budget negotiations it is well-known that the net national position is the most crucial aspect of the intergovernmental bargaining that leads to the agreement of the Multi-annual Financial Framework, so that there would be a certain logic in translating this into how cohesion funding is distributed.

Cohesion policy has traditionally relied on direct grants to programmes and projects, but has come under increasing pressures to employ other forms of financial instruments: in essence, this means variations on loans. The experience of the fifteen regions is that grants work well enough, but that other instruments both create more uncertainty and can complicate policy implementation. However, as economic development moves away from some of the investment in basic infrastructure that is, in many regions, a crucial step on the development ladder, the merits of more diverse forms of financing are bound to come under fresh scrutiny. In encouraging enterprise development, for example, grants to subsidise SMEs can undoubtedly help, but may lead to dependency on subsidy that is at odds with economic resilience. There are also questions about the (as yet) unproven effectiveness and efficiency of financial instruments such as loans, guarantees and equity in the Cohesion policy domain.

Rhetoric about a results orientation dominated the 2014–2020 reform debate and may be worthy in principle, but for a policy to be results-oriented it needs to have clarity of purpose. Coordination with national policies delivered by central, regional and local tiers of government lies at the heart of Cohesion policy, and there also has to be engagement with other stakeholders, notably in the business sector. The potential for incompatibility in goals is obvious, but there are also tricky questions around incentives and penalties, especially in a context in which more binding conditionality is imposed. Regions risk being penalised for infractions by central government, while subnational governments may lack incentives for fiscal discipline. It follows that great care has to be taken in the design of effective mechanisms for imposing discipline in policy implementation, if adverse incentives are to be avoided.

In many of the recent debates on reforming Cohesion policy, there has been a propensity to focus unduly on the small things rather than addressing first the big things on which the small things depend. The fundamental question, from which everything else should follow, should be what the policy ought to be doing, where and for whom. Until it is convincingly answered, there is an acute risk that key principles will be lost in the details. In this regard, evaluation is vital, but is not always done ideally. If ex post evaluations are done prematurely, for example, before programmes are concluded, they will inevitably be hampered by data shortcomings and will be prone to be too broad in scope. Here, the discussion in chapters 2 and 3 and the results presented in chapters 5–7 are instructive, demonstrating how many programme strategies were often not linked to sound analyses of needs or evaluation evidence, were not based on robust monitoring data, or gave inadequate consideration of the time frame over which interventions could be assessed.

FINAL MESSAGES FROM THE STUDY

The research summarised in this volume provides clear evidence to support the direction of Cohesion policy in 2014–2020, specifically with respect to the emphasis on conditionalities, the new results-orientation, the enhanced performance framework and the promotion of capacity-building both as a thematic priority and the creation of administrative capacity units in DG Regio and DG Empl of the European Commission. These are areas where our findings show successive generations of programmes to have been deficient. However, while the principles of these changes are supported by the research, the practical obstacles are significant.

First, the study demonstrates that changing policy priorities and management practices takes a long time, certainly more than one programme period. The resistance by some member states to the new regulations for 2014–2020 as part of the negotiations, and the caution on the part of programme authorities in responding to the Commission's expectations, suggests that achieving the necessary revolutionary change in performance under the new programmes will be difficult.

Second, the study has identified a long list of lessons that apply to every stage of the programme cycle. They point to deficits in the conceptual approach to programming, strategic planning techniques, analytical methods to support project selection, and the quality or focus of monitoring and evaluation. This calls for a major effort to build administrative capacity and promote learning.

Of all the changes required, perhaps the most important is to encourage and support a more sophisticated approach to long-term strategic analysis and planning, drawing on theory and practice in ways that challenge conventional thinking, and rooted in a detailed understanding of the distinctive strengths and weaknesses of individual regions. The recommended approach to smart specialisation for post-2014 programming may be worthy in principle, but it presupposes a level of competence and experience that (this study suggests) does not exist everywhere. While the programming for 2014–2020 has seen at least some steps forward in improving the performance of programmes, a more realistic timescale for implementing the lessons of this study is to look forward to the post-2020 programme period and a strategy to raise awareness and invest in knowledge, skills and expertise. Taking this kind of long-term study perspective for each member state could provide a road map on what Cohesion policy has achieved (or not) in individual countries and regions, where the problems lie and how specific improvements might be achieved.

NOTE

1. TAIEX REGIO PEER 2 PEER is designed to share expertise between bodies that manage funding under the European Regional Development Fund and the Cohesion Fund. See http://ec.europa.eu/regional_policy/en/policy/how/ improving-investment/taiex-regio-peer-2-peer.

Bibliography

Affuso, Antonio, Roberta Capello and Ugo Fratesi. 2011. 'Globalization and Competitive Strategies in European Vulnerable Regions'. *Regional Studies* 45 (5): 657–75. doi:10.1080/00343401003614290.

Amin, Ash, and John Tomaney. 1995. 'The Regional Dilemma in a Neo-Liberal Europe'. *European Urban and Regional Studies* 2 (2): 171–88. doi:10.1177/096977649500200205.

Applica, Ismeri Europa, and WiiW. 2009. *Ex post evaluation of Cohesion Policy programmes 2007-2013, financed by the European Regional Development Fund (ERDF) and Cohesion Fund (CF), Work Package One: Synthesis report.*

Bachtler, John. 2001. 'Where Is Regional Policy Going? Changing Concepts of Regional Policy'. Paper to the 22nd International Meeting of the Regional Policy Research Consortium of Nine European Regional Policy Departments, Ross Priory, Loch Lomondside, October 7–9.

Bachtler, John, and Carlos Mendez. 2010. 'The Reform of Cohesion Policy after 2013: More Concentration, Better Performance and Better Governance?' *IQ-Net Thematic Paper* 26 (2). Glasgow: European Policies Research Centre, University of Strathclyde.

Bachtler, John, and Carlos Mendez. 2016. 'Cohesion Policy Reform and the Evolving Role of the Council'. In *Handbook on Cohesion Policy in the EU*, edited by Simona Piattonia and Laura Polverari, chapter 8. Cheltenham, UK; Northampton, MA, USA: Edward Elgar.

Bachtler, John, Carlos Mendez and Fiona Wishlade. 2013. *EU Cohesion Policy and European Integration: The Dynamics of EU Budget and Regional Policy Reform*. Farnham: Ashgate.

Bachtler, John, and Grzegorz Gorzelak. 2007. 'Reforming EU Cohesion Policy: A Reappraisal of the Performance of the Structural Funds'. *Policy Studies* 28 (4): 309–26. doi:10.1080/01442870701640682.

Bachtler, John, Iain Begg, Laura Polverari and David Charles. 2013. *Evaluation of the Main Achievements of Cohesion Policy Programmes and Projects over the Longer Term in 15 Selected Regions (from 1989-1993 Programme Period to the Present* (2011.CE.16.B.AT.015). Final Report to the European Commission (DG Regio), European Policies Research Centre, University of Strathclyde (Glasgow) and London School of Economics.

Bachtler, John, Ruth Downes, Rona Michie, Mary Louise Rooney and Sandra Taylor. 2000. 'New Structural Fund Programming: Laying the Foundations'. *IQ-Net Thematic Paper* 6 (2). Glasgow: European Policies Research Centre, University of Strathclyde.

Bachtler, John, and Sandra Taylor. 1999. *Objective 2: Experiences, Lessons and Policy Implications.* Final Report to the European Commission (DG Regio).

Bachtler, John, and Sara Davies. 2010. 'The Geography of the Crisis in Western Europe: National and Regional Impacts and Policy Responses'. In *Financial Crisis in Central and Eastern Europe—from Similarity to Diversity*, edited by Grzegor Gorzelak and Chor-Ching Goh, 224–35. Warsaw: Scholar.

Barca, Fabrizio. 2009. *An Agenda for a Reformed Cohesion Policy: A Place-Based Approach to Meeting European Union Challenges and Expectations.* Independent Report prepared at the request of Danuta Hübner, Commissioner for Regional Policy, EC.

Becker, Sascha O., Peter H. Egger and Maximilian Von Ehrlich. 2010. 'Going NUTS: The Effect of EU Structural Funds on Regional Performance'. *Journal of Public Economics* 94: 578–90. doi:10.1016/j.jpubeco.2010.06.006.

Begg, Iain. 2010. 'Cohesion or Confusion: A Policy Searching for Objectives'. *Journal of European Integration* 32 (1): 77–96. doi:10.1080/07036330903375115.

Begg, Iain. 2016. 'The Economic Theory of Cohesion Policy'. In *Handbook on Cohesion Policy in the EU*, edited by Simona Piattoni and Laura Polverari, chapter 3. Cheltenham, UK; Northampton, MA, USA: Edward Elgar.

Begg, Iain, Corrado Macchiarelli, John Bachtler, Carlos Mendez and Fiona Wishlade. 2014. *European Economic Governance and Cohesion Policy.* Report to the European Parliament Committee on Regional Development. Brussels: European Parliament.

Berkowitz, Peter. 2015. '*A More Effective and Efficient Policy? Assessing the Implementation of the Reform of Cohesion Policy*'. Paper for the Second EU Cohesion Policy Conference 'Challenges for the New Cohesion Policy 2014–2020. An Academic and Policy Debate', Riga, Latvia, February 4–6.

Biehl, Dieter. 1991. 'The Role of Infrastructure in Regional Development'. In *Infrastructure and Regional Development*, edited by Roger Vickerman, 9–35. London: Pion.

Boldrin, Michele, and Fabio Canova. 2001. 'Inequality and Convergence: Reconsidering European Regional Policies'. *Economic Policy* 32: 207–53. doi:10.1111/1468-0327.00074.

Bondonio, Daniele, and Alberto Martini. 2012. *Counterfactual Impact Evaluation of Cohesion Policy: Impact and Cost-Effectiveness of Investment Subsidies in Italy.* Final Report to DG Regional Policy 'Counterfactual Impact Evaluation of Cohesion Policy'. Torino: Associazione per lo Sviluppo della Valutazione e l'Analisi delle Politiche Pubbliche.

Bradley, John, and Gerhard Untiedt. 2009. *Analysis of EU Cohesion Policy 2000-2006 Using the CSHM: Aggregate Impacts and Inter-Country Comparisons.* Report to the European Commission. Dublin.

Bradley, John, Gerhard Untiedt and Timo Mitze. 2007. *Analysis of the Impact of Cohesion Policy: A Note Explaining the HERMIN-Based Simulations.* Report to the European Commission. Dublin.

Bristow, Gillian. 2010. 'Resilient Regions: Re-'Place'ing Regional Competitiveness'. *Cambridge Journal of Regions, Economy and Society* 3 (1): 153–67. doi:10.1093/cjres/rsp030.

Camagni, Roberto. 1991a. 'Interregional Disparities in the European Community: Structure and Performance of Objective One Regions in the 1980s'. Paper presented to the North American Regional Science Conference, New Orleans, November 6–9.

Camagni, Roberto. 1991b. 'Regional Deindustrialization and Revitalization Processes in Italy'. In *Industrial Change and Regional Economic Transformation*, edited by Lloyd Rodwin and Hidehiko Sazanami, 137–67. London: HarperCollins.

Cappelen, Aadne, Fulvio Castellacci, Jan Fagerberg and Bart Verspagen. 2003. 'The Impact of EU Regional Support on Growth and Convergence in the European Union'. *Journal of Common Market Studies* 41: 621–44. doi:10.1111/1468-5965.00438.

Casavola, Paola. 2009. *Operational Rules and Results in Cohesion Policy Programmes: Analysis and Proposals for Conditionalities.* Report Working Paper written in the context of the report 'An Agenda for a reformed Cohesion Policy', January 2009.

Centre for Industrial Studies (CSIL) and DKM Economic Consultants. 2012. *Ex Post Evaluation of Investment Projects Co-Financed by the ERDF or Cohesion Fund in the Period 1994–1999: Ten Projects Observed.* Final Report to the European Commission (DG Regional Policy). Milan and Dublin.

Charles, David, Frederike Gross and John Bachtler. 2012. '"Smart Specialisation" and Cohesion Policy—a Strategy for All Regions?' *IQ-Net Thematic Paper* 30 (2). Glasgow: European Policies Research Centre, University of Strathclyde.

Cheshire, Paul, and Stefano Magrini. 2000. 'Endogenous Processes in European Regional Growth: Convergence and Policy'. *Growth and Change* 31 (4): 455–79. doi:10.1111/0017-4815.00140.

Ciffolilli, Andrea, Lydia Greunz, Andrea Naldini, Terry Ward and Enrico Wolleb. 2013. *Expert Evaluation Network: Synthesis of National Reports 2012*. A report to the European Commission Directorate-General for Regional and Urban Policy, January 2013.

Creţu, Corina. 2015. Speech at the 55th Congress of the European Regional Science Association in Lisbon, Portugal, 28 August 2015.

Criscuolo, Chiara, Ralf Martin, Henry Overman and John Van Reenen. 2012. *The Causal Effects of an Industrial Policy*. NBER Working Papers 17842. National Bureau of Economic Research, Cambridge, MA.

CSES (Centre for Strategy and Evaluation Services). 2003. *Ex Post Evaluation of 1994-99 Objective 2 Programmes*. Synthesis Report to the Directorate General for Regional Policy, European Commission. Sevenoaks: Centre for Strategy and Evaluation Services.

Dall'Erba, Sandy. 2005. 'Distribution of Regional Income and Regional Funds in Europe 1989-1999: An Exploratory Spatial Data Analysis'. *The Annals of Regional Science* 39 (1): 121–48. doi:10.1007/s00168-004-0199-4.

Davies, Sara. 2011. 'Regional Resilience in the 2008-2010 Downturn: Comparative Evidence from European Countries'. *Cambridge Journal of Regions, Economy and Society* 4 (3): 369–82. doi:10.1093/cjres/rsr019.

Davies, Sara. 2014. 'Assessment of Effectiveness'. In *Balance of Competences Cohesion Review: Literature Review on EU Cohesion Policy*, by Laura Polverari and John Bachtler with Sara Davies, Stefan Kah, Carlos Mendez, Rona Michie and Heidi Vironen. Final Report to the Department for Business, Innovation and Skills. Glasgow: European Policies Research Centre, University of Strathclyde.

de la Fuente, Angel, and Xavier Vives. 1995. 'Infrastructure and Education as Instruments of Regional Policy: Evidence from Spain'. *Economic Policy* 10: 11–51. doi:10.2307/1344537.

DG Regio. 2011. *Outcome Indicators and Targets: Towards a New System of Monitoring and Evaluation in EE Cohesion Policy*. Prepared by an expert group within DG REGIO. Brussels: DG Regio.

ECOTEC. 2003. *Ex-Post Evaluation of Objective 1, 1994-1999*. A Final Report to the Directorate General for Regional Policy, European Commission. Birmingham: ECOTEC Research & Consulting Limited.

European Commission. 1997. 'Agenda 2000: For a Stronger and Wider Union'. *Bulletin of the European Communities* 5 (97): 5–78.

European Commission. 1999. *Indicators for Monitoring and Evaluation: An Indicative Methodology*. DG Regio Working Paper 3. Brussels: European Commission.

European Commission. 2011. Guidance Document on *Monitoring and Evaluation of European Cohesion Policy, European Regional Development Fund and Cohesion Fund: Concepts and Recommendations*. The Programme Period 2014–2020. Draft November 2011. European Commission, DG Regio.

European Commission. 2013a. 'EVALSED: The Resource for the Evaluation of Socio-Economic Development—Evaluation Guide'. Last modified September 16. http://ec.europa.eu/regional_policy/en/information/publications/evaluations-guidance-documents/2013/evalsed-the-resource-for-the-evaluation-of-socio-economic-development-evaluation-guide.

European Commission. 2013b. *Results Indicators 2014+: Report on Pilot Tests in 23 Regions/OPs across 15 MS of the EU*. Brussels: DG Regio.

European Commission. 2013c. *Cohesion Policy: Strategic Report 2013 on Programme Implementation 2007-2013*. Report from the Commission to the European Parliament, the Council, the European Economic and Social Committee and the Committee of the Regions. Commission Staff Working Document. Brussels: European Commission.

European Commission. 2014. *Investment for Jobs and Growth: Promoting Development and Good Governance in EU Regions and Cities*. Sixth Report on Economic, Social and Territorial Cohesion. Brussels: European Commission.

European Commission. 2015a. 'Evaluations of the 2007-2013 Programming Period'. Last modified May 6. http://ec.europa.eu/regional_policy/en/policy/evaluations/ec/2007-2013.

European Commission. 2015b. *On Steps Towards Completing Economic and Monetary Union*. Communication from the Commission to the European Parliament, the Council and the European Central Bank, COM(2015) 600 final, 21.10.2015. Brussels: European Commission.

European Commission. 2015c. 'TAIEX REGIO PEER 2 PEER'. Last modified March 16. http://ec.europa.eu/regional_policy/en/policy/how/improving-investment/taiex-regio-peer-2-peer.

European Court of Auditors. 2014. *EU-Funded Airport Infrastructures: Poor Value for Money*. Special Report No 21/2014. European Union, Luxembourg.

Eurostat. 2015. http://ec.europa.eu/eurostat.

Farole, Thomas, Andrés Rodríguez-Pose and Michael Storper. 2010. 'Human Geography and the Institutions That Underlie Economic Growth'. *Progress in Human Geography* 35 (1): 58–80. doi:10.1177/0309132510372005.

Foray, Dominique, Paul A. David and Bronwyn H. Hall. 2011. *Smart Specialization: From Academic Idea to Political Instrument, the Surprising Career of a Concept and the Difficulties Involved in its Implementation*. MTEI Working Paper 2011-001. Lausanne: EPFL (École Polytechnique Fédérale de Lausanne).

Hagen, Tobias, and Philipp Mohl. 2008. *Which Is the Right Dose of EU Cohesion Policy for Economic Growth?* Discussion Paper No. 08-104. Mannheim: ZEW (Centre for European Economic Research).

Hagen, Tobias, and Philipp Mohl. 2011. 'Econometric Evaluation of EU Cohesion Policy: A Survey'. In *International Handbook on the Economics of Integration: Factor Mobility, Agriculture, Environment and Quantitative Studies* 3, edited by Miroslav Jovanovic, 343–70. Cheltenham and Northampton: Edward Elgar.

Hart, Mark. 2007. 'Evaluating EU Regional Policy: How Might We Understand the Causal Connections between Interventions and Outcomes More Effectively?' *Policy Studies* 28 (4): 295–308. doi:10.1080/01442870701640666.

Hart, Mark, and Karen Bonner. 2011. *Data-Linking and Impact Evaluation in Northern Ireland*. Final report to the European Commission (DG Regional Policy). Birmingham: Aston Business School.

Honohan, Patrick, ed. 1997. *EU Structural Funds in Ireland: A Mid-Term Evaluation of the CSF 1994-99*. Policy Research Series 31. Dublin: Economic and Social Research Institute (ESRI).

in t'Veld, Jan. 2007. *The Potential Impact of the Fiscal Transfers under the EU Cohesion Policy Programme*. ECFIN European Economy Economic Papers 283. Brussels: European Commission.

Juncker, Jean-Claude, with Donald Tusk, Jeroen Dijsselbloem, Mario Draghi and Martin Schulz. 2015. *Completing Europe's Economic and Monetary Union*. Five Presidents' Report. Brussels: European Commission.

Kitching, John. 2006. 'A Burden on Business? Reviewing the Evidence Base on Regulation and Small-Business Performance'. *Environment and Planning C: Government and Policy* 24: 799–814. doi:10.1068/c0619.

Landabaso, Mikel, and Alasdair Reid. 1999. 'Developing Regional Innovation Strategies: The European Commission as Animateur'. In *Regional Innovation Strategies: The Challenge for Less-Favoured Regions*, edited by Kevin Morgan and Claire Nauwelaers, 1–18. London: The Stationery Office.

Leuuw, Frans L. 2003. 'Reconstructing Program Theories: Methods Available and Problems to Be Solved'. *American Journal of Evaluation* 24 (1): 5–20. doi:10.1177/109821400302400102.

Leuuw, Frans L. 2012. 'Linking Theory-Based Evaluation and Contribution Analysis: Three Problems and a Few Solutions'. *Evaluation* 18 (3): 348–63. doi:10.1177/1356389012452051.

LSE Enterprise Ltd, Vision & Value, Red2Red Consultores, Expanzió Consulting Ltd, and Deutschland Denken! e.V. 2010. *The Ex Post Evaluation of the European Social Fund (2000-2006)*. Final Report to the European Commission.

Malecki, Edward J. 1997. *Technology and Economic Development: The Dynamics of Local, Regional and National Change*. London: Addison Wesley Longman.

Mayne, John. 2011. 'Contribution Analysis: Addressing Cause and Effect'. In *Evaluating the Complex: Attribution, Contribution and Beyond*, edited by Kim Forss, Mita Marra and Robert Schwartz, 53–96. New Brunswick: Transaction Publishers.

Mendez, Carlos. 2011. 'The Lisbonization of EU Cohesion Policy: A Successful Case of Experimentalist Governance?' *European Planning Studies* 19 (3): 519–37. doi:10.1080/09654313.2011.548368.

Mendez, Carlos, and John Bachtler. 2015. 'Permanent Revolution in Cohesion Policy: Restarting the Reform Debate'. *European Policy Research Paper* 93. Glasgow: European Policies Research Centre, University of Stathclyde.

Mendez, Carlos, John Bachtler and Fiona Wishlade. 2011. 'Setting the Stage for the Reform of Cohesion Policy after 2013'. *European Policy Research Paper* 77. Glasgow: European Policies Research Centre, University of Strathclyde.

Midelfart-Knarvik, Karen Helene, and Henry G. Overman. 2002. 'Delocation and European Integration: Is Structural Spending Justified?' *Economic Policy* 17 (35): 321–59. doi:10.1111/1468-0327.00091.

Mohl, Philipp, and Tobias Hagen. 2010. 'Do EU Structural Funds Promote Regional Growth? New Evidence from Various Panel Data Approaches'. *Regional Science and Urban Economics* 40 (5): 353–65. doi:10.1016/j.regsciurbeco.2010.03.005.

Mole, Kevin F., Mark Hart, Stephen Roper and David S. Saal. 2009. 'Assessing the Effectiveness of Business Support Services in England: Evidence from a Theory-Based Evaluation'. *International Small Business Journal* 27 (5): 557–82. doi:10.1177/0266242609338755.

Morgan, Kevin. 1997. 'The Learning Region: Institutions, Innovation and Regional Renewal'. *Regional Studies* 31 (5): 491–503. doi:10.1080/00343409750132289.

Nordregio. 2009. *The Potential for Regional Policy Instruments (2007-13) to Contribute to the Lisbon and Göteborg Objectives for Growth, Jobs and Sustainable Development*. Final Report to the European Commission, Directorate-General for Regional Policy. Stockholm: Nordregio.

OECD (Organisation for Economic Growth and Development). 2009. *Regions Matter: Economic Recovery, Innovation and Sustainable Growth*. Paris: Organisation for Economic Growth and Development.

Olejniczak, Karol. 2009. 'Mini-Case Study: Building the Evaluation System in Poland'. In *Ex Post Evaluation of Cohesion Policy Programmes 2000-06 Co-financed by ERDF. Work Package 11: Management and Implementation System for Cohesion Policy*. Glasgow: European Policies Research Centre, University of Strathclyde.

Pawson, Hal, and Keith Kintrea. 2002. 'Part of the Problem or Part of the Solution? Social Housing Allocation Policies and Social Exclusion in Britain'. *Journal of Social Policy*, 31 (4): 643–67. doi:10.1017/S0047279402006797.

Pike, Andy, Andrés Rodríguez-Pose and John Tomaney. 2011. *Handbook of Local and Regional Development*. London; New York: Routledge.

Polverari, Laura, and John Bachtler, with Sara Davies, Stefan Kah, Carlos Mendez, Rona Michie and Heidi Vironen. 2014. *Balance of Competences Cohesion Review: Literature Review on EU Cohesion Policy*. Final Report to the Department for Business, Innovation and Skills. Glasgow: European Policies Research Centre, University of Strathclyde.

Rodríguez-Pose, Andrés. 2001. 'Is R&D Investment in Lagging Areas of Europe Worthwhile? Theory and Empirical Evidence'. *Papers in Regional Science* 80 (3): 275–95. doi:10.1111/j.1435-5597.2001.tb01800.x.

Rodríguez-Pose, Andrés. 2013. 'Do Institutions Matter for Regional Development?' *Regional Studies* 47 (7): 1034–47. doi:10.1080/00343404.2012.748978.

Rodríguez-Pose, Andrés, and Ugo Fratesi. 2004. 'Between Development and Social Policies: The Impact of European Structural Funds in Objective 1 Regions'. *Regional Studies* 38 (1): 97–113. doi:10.1080/0034340031000 1632226.

Sapir, André. 2003. *An Agenda for a Growing Europe: Making the EU Economic System Deliver*. Report of an Independent High-Level Study Group established on the initiative of the President of the European Commission. Brussels.

SRDE. 2005. *Le Schéma régional de développement* économique *(SRDE), adopté par le Conseil régional le 24 novembre 2005*, Région Nord-Pas de Calais, Lille.

Storper, Michael. 1995. 'Competitiveness Policy Options: The Technology–Regions Connection'. *Growth and Change* 26 (2): 285–308. doi:10.1111/j.1468-2257.1995.tb00172.x.

SWECO. 2008. *Final Report—ERDF and CF Regional Expenditure*. Contract No 2007.CE.16.0.AT.036. Stockholm: SWECO International AB.

Taylor, Sandra, John Bachtler, Francois Josserand and Laura Polverari. 2004. 'Achieving the Aspirations of the 2000-06 Programming Period'. *IQ-Net Thematic Paper* 14 (2). Glasgow: European Policies Research Centre, University of Strathclyde.

Trzciński, Rafał. 2011. 'Impact of Direct Subsidies on SMEs'. In *Towards Innovative Economy: Effects of Grants to Enterprises in Poland*, edited by Jacek Pokorski, 215–24. Warsaw: Polish Agency for Enterprise Development.

Varga, Janos, and Jan in t'Veld. 2010. *The Potential Impact of EU Cohesion Policy Spending in the 2007-13 Programming Period: A Model-Based Analysis*. ECFIN European Economy Economic Papers 422. Brussels: European Commission.

Ward, Terry, Lydia Greunz and Sara Botti. 2012. *Ex-Post Evaluation of the Cohesion Fund (Including Former ISPA) in the 2000-2006 Period.* Synthesis Report to the European Commission (DG Regional Policy), Applica.

Weiss, Carol H. 1997. 'How Can Theory-Based Evaluation Make Greater Headway?' *Evaluation Review* 21 (4): 501–24. doi:10.1177/0193841X9702100405.

World Bank. 2009. *World Development Report 2009: Reshaping Economic Geography.* Washington, DC: World Bank.

Index

www.ingramcontent.com/pod-product-compliance
Lightning Source LLC
Chambersburg PA
CBHW021820270326
41932CB00007B/274

* 9 7 8 1 7 8 3 4 8 7 2 2 6 *